hievement

LIBRARY OF MEDIEVAL CIVILIZATION
EDITED BY JOAN EVANS AND
PROFESSOR CHRISTOPHER BROOKE

The

GEORGE ZARNECKI

Monastic Achievement

McGRAW-HILL BOOK COMPANY · NEW YORK

Frontispiece St Guthlac receiving the tonsure at Repton Abbey, a late twelfth-century drawing from the Guthlac Roll

Library of Congress Catalog Card Number: 79-175186

Printed and bound in Great Britain

07-072736-8 clothbound
07-072735-x paperbound

Contents

Preface

As originally written, my text was intended to outline the artistic achievement of medieval monasteries in the West, coming as it did in the wake of the great reforms of the tenth and eleventh centuries. The decision to publish my chapter from *The Flowering of the Middle Ages* (1966) as a separate book presented me with the difficult problem of making it more self-sufficient. With this aim in mind, I expanded the text by adding a very brief history of early monasticism and discussing some of its artistic achievements before the eleventh century. However, the present book is not a history of monasticism or a history of monastic art, but is a little of both. It is my hope that readers will subsequently turn to more specialized books, of which a selection is listed in the Bibliography.

The history of monastic art is still to be written. The material is enormous and often very fragmentary and insufficiently documented, but the greatest difficulty in dealing with it is our ignorance on such matters as what was due to the monks themselves and what merely to monastic patronage. I have tried, I hope without being dogmatic on this controversial issue, to illustrate examples of both. What I have written is based largely on the research of others, too numerous to be acknowledged individually. My greatest debt and gratitude goes to my friends, Joan Evans, who originally invited me to join her team writing *The Flowering of the Middle Ages*, and Christopher Brooke who, as the editor of the present series, read my text, making critical suggestions for improvements. Any shortcomings, however, are due to me alone. I am also grateful to Emily Lane and Vanessa Whinney of Thames and Hudson for their help in selecting new illustrations and to Kathy Trudgett and Susan Catling who helped with the manuscript and proofs.

G.Z.

Foreword
to the Original Edition

Fifty years ago history was mainly studied in school and university, and as a consequence by the educated reader, in terms of wars, political alliances and constitutional developments. Its base was properly in written documents, and even social history was not envisaged in other than documentary terms. Eight half-tone illustrations were enough for any historical work and most were not illustrated at all.

Now, at least for the general reader, all is changed. Schoolmasters attempt to give some visual background to their history lessons; occasionally even a professor of history may show a few slides. Professional historians and archivists rightly continue to study every facet of their subject in documented detail, but for most people 'history' has become a much more general matter, that provides them with a background to what they see and what they read. For them, at least, historians must so interpret the documents as to make them reveal the life of the past rather than its battles and its political machinations.

This change is due less to the professional historians themselves than to a change of view in the reading public: a change that can only be paralleled in the second half of the nineteenth century when trains and steamers made it easy to travel and everyone began to know their Europe. That time produced its Ruskin and its Viollet-le-Duc, its Lasteyrie and its Henry Adams; but we forget that Ruskin had to draw, or to engage others to draw for him, the things he wrote and talked about, and that Viollet-le-Duc was never able to reproduce a photograph.

In our own day a new wave of travel by car and plane has been accompanied by incredible developments in photography and in reproduction. Black and white photographs and half-tone blocks revolutionized the study of architecture and art at the end of the nineteenth century, and the great archaeological discoveries of the day made the general public willing to accept an object or a building *pari passu* with a written document. In our own time colour photographs and colour plates have enriched these studies in a way that would have seemed miraculous to Ruskin.

Moreover, though education remains astonishingly bookish, our recreations have trained our eyes. An experienced and successful lecturer of 1900 said that a slide must remain on the screen for at least a minute to give the audience time to take it in. Now, the cinema screen and the television set have trained us in visual nimbleness, and we 'see' much more quickly. . . .

Somewhere about 1100 it seems as if Europe settled on an even keel. In England the Norman dynasty had established itself militarily and administratively. In France Philip I had established a rival kingdom, the Cluniac reform had revivified religious life, and the Crusades had started on their way. In Germany Henry IV was establishing the Empire on a firmer basis. In Italy Pope Gregory VII had lost his fight against the Emperor, but had gained new spiritual force for Rome. In Spain Alfonso VI of Castile had made Toledo the capital of Christian Spain, and the Cid had conquered Valencia. In the Eastern Empire the Comneni had suffered the inroads first of the Normans and then of the Crusaders; the weight of power was shifting westward. In Europe it is fair to say that a measure of stability had been achieved, in which the forces of feudalism, monasticism, scholastic philosophy and civic growth could work together to make the history of the Middle Ages.

To make that history more real to the ordinary reader is our purpose. The authors have not here published unknown documents, unknown monuments or unknown works of art, but have tried by the interpretation of what is known to make the Christian civilization of Europe in the Middle Ages more significant and more comprehensible to the readers of today. The keyword to our conception of history is civilization.

JOAN EVANS

Chapter One

Monastic Origins

The idea of the ascetic life as a means of purifying the soul is characteristic of many religions, and Christianity was no exception. Asceticism was implied in the Gospels, for Jesus is quoted in St Mark (VIII, 34) as saying, 'Whosoever will come after me, let him deny himself, and take up his cross, and follow me', and in St John (XII, 25), 'He that loveth his life shall lose it; and he that hateth his life in this world shall keep it unto life eternal.' Jesus had recommended self-denial in explicit terms: fasting, the renunciation of all possessions ('If thou will be perfect, go and sell that thou hast, and give to the poor, and thou shalt have treasure in heaven: and come and follow me', St Matthew XIX, 21), and chastity ('and there be eunuchs, which have made themselves eunuchs for the kingdom of heaven's sake', St Matthew XIX, 12).

Inspired by these ideals, self-imposed denial of various kinds was practised within the framework of Christian family life from the earliest times; but, gradually and especially in the periods of persecution, this asceticism took more extreme and harsh forms, and became incompatible with normal life and everyday occupations. Thus began the practice of seeking isolation in deserts and mountains, or at least outside cities, where there was little contact with the rest of the world. This practice became particularly common in Egypt from the third century onwards, and it was also in Egypt that colonies of hermits, living separately in caves or primitive structures, but in close proximity to each other for mutual support and encouragement, began to appear. Monasticism was born from such loosely organized communities of 'Desert Fathers'. But it would be a mistake to think that coenobites (the religious living in a community) replaced the hermits and recluses altogether. Throughout the Middle Ages, both in the East and West, many individuals preferred a solitary, eremitical life to an organized, communal one. Many saints spent part of their lives as hermits.

1 The founder of Western monasticism, St Benedict: a late ninth-century fresco in S. Crisogono in Trastevere, Rome

2, 3 Two of the Church leaders who influenced monastic thought, portrayed in eleventh-century manuscripts from the abbey of Christchurch, Canterbury. *Above:* St Pachomius (receiving the Easter Tables). *Right:* St Augustine, holding his *City of God*

The man who first organized the hermits' colonies into quasi-monastic communities, early in the fourth century, was St Anthony, himself a hermit, who spent many years in complete isolation in the Egyptian desert. But the true founder of Christian monasticism was St Pachomius (d. 346), who established, in southern Egypt, a number of monasteries for men and one for women. These were based on written rules for a life of common prayer and work, in conditions of great austerity. All these monasteries were dependent on the head-house at Tabenissi, and the abbot of the head-house appointed the other abbots and exercised general control over them. Many centuries later, the Cluniac Order adopted a similar hierarchic organization.

The monasticism organized by St Pachomius spread throughout Egypt, Ethiopia and Asia Minor and, thanks to the translation of the Rule into Latin by St Jerome in 404, its influence was also felt in the West. Originating in harsh desert conditions, and during the time of the decline of the Roman Empire and of religious controversies and heresies, Pachomian monasticism was characterized by excessive ascetic zeal. Transplanted to Asia Minor, its character was

modified by a relaxation of the austerities and a greater stress on communal activities and charitable works. The change was due to St Basil (*c.* 330–79), who knew Egyptian monasteries well and who himself spent six years as a hermit. Highly educated and learned, he devised a monastic rule known as the Basilian, which, with some changes, still survives in the Orthodox Church. Although strict, it avoids the ascetic extreme of St Pachomius. A Basilian monk was to lead a life of prayer and work, in poverty, chastity and in obedience to his superiors. The hours for liturgical prayer were laid down, as were those of work in the fields and in various crafts. The monasteries were also to run hospitals, orphanages and schools. The blending of asceticism with an active, useful life assured the Basilian monasteries a great popularity, which spread throughout the vast territories under Byzantine rule or influence. In southern Italy, which was for many centuries under Byzantine domination, Basilian monks settled in great numbers, fleeing from Egypt and Asia Minor at the time of the Arab conquests and from Greece during the persecutions following the iconoclastic controversy. Purely Byzantine buildings, such as at Stilo in Calabria and, above all, the numerous underground chapels with frescoes found in Sicily, Calabria and Apulia, testify to a once very active monastic life in those territories, particularly flourishing during the tenth and eleventh centuries.

The knowledge of Basilian monasticism in the West came not

only by way of southern Italy. The works of St Basil were translated into Latin by Rufinus of Aquileia (d. 410) and, of course, many Western churchmen, traders and others travelled to the East and thus had first-hand information about monastic life there. Rufinus himself visited Egypt and Jerusalem.

The craving for an ascetic life in the service of God was not confined to the Eastern part of the Empire, and, in the course of the fourth century, monasteries appeared throughout the West. St 3 Augustine visited a number of them in Italy and, on his return to Africa, founded one himself in Tagaste, his birth-place. The Rule on which it was based was revived late in the eleventh century by Regular (or Augustinian) Canons. The monasteries which St Augustine knew in Italy were not only for men but also for women. These Italian monasteries, as well as those in Gaul and Spain, had come into being under the influence of those in the East. They were usually established by prominent churchmen, such as St Ambrose at Milan, or by rich converts like St Paulinus and his wife, who built the celebrated monastery at Cimitile near Nola in Campania, around the martyrium of St Felix. Paulinus, who later became bishop of Nola, had among his friends many prominent Christians who were also founders of monasteries. One of these was St Martin of Tours, who founded Ligugé and Marmoutier. Provence was particularly rich in early monasteries, which included Lérins, founded by St Honoratus in 395, on a small island off 4 Cannes now known as St Honorat. It was a centre of learning and of missionary activity, and it was here that St Patrick, 'Apostle of the Irish', received his education. Another important monastery in Provence was St Victor at Marseilles, founded in about the year 415 by John Cassian, described cryptically as being 'natione Scytha', formerly a monk in Bethlehem and deacon in Constantinople. His famous Rule is contained in the book *Institutiones*: it had a decisive influence on St Benedict, as did his other work, the *Collationes* (Conferences), containing his conversations with the leaders of Eastern monasticism: this became daily reading for Benedictine monks (St Benedict's *Regula*, Chapter XLII). In large cities, and especially in Rome, a peculiar development took place, which involved groups of monks serving as the choir and often as the clergy in large basilicas. In later centuries, Regular Canons took the place of these monks, whose function had been primarily liturgical.

This early development of monastic life was crowned by the work of St Benedict who is, quite rightly, considered the true father of Western monasticism.

1, 5, 12

Early monasticism in Western Europe was characterized by a great diversity in the rules on which individual foundations were based. One early foundation, at Monte Cassino, through the merits of its rule and through historical circumstances, became a model which, in time, all other monasteries imitated. The Rule, known as the Benedictine, was initiated by a man who is to Western monasticism what St Pachomius and St Basil were to Eastern. St Benedict (c. 480–c. 550) began his religious career as a hermit in a cave near Subiaco. As in so many instances before and since, the sanctity of the hermit attracted many followers, and for these St Benedict formed twelve monasteries, each consisting of twelve monks. But he was eventually driven away by the jealousy and intrigues of a local priest, and established, in about 529, a monastery at Monte Cassino, halfway between Rome and Naples. His sister, St Scholastica, followed him and founded a convent for women at nearby Plombariola.

4 The island of St Honorat. The monastic buildings on the left shore are on the site of St Honoratus's abbey, founded in 395

5–7 MONTE CASSINO: BENEDICTINE BEGINNINGS *Left:* St Benedict hands his Rule to a group of monks (twelfth century). *Below:* the abbey about 1075, some 550 years after its foundation. Extensive residential and service buildings are grouped around a cloister south of the church. *Right:* the ornate pulpit and Paschal candlestick inside the church appear in this drawing of a service, from an Exultet roll made for Monte Cassino in the eleventh century

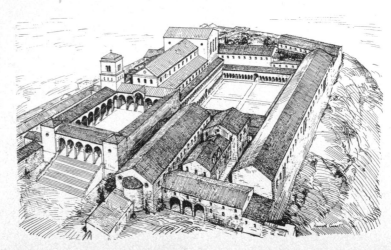

8 *Right:* the church
of Cassiodorus's
foundation of
Vivarium (540),
St Martin, is shown
with stylized towers
in an eighth-century
manuscript. In the
foreground is the
monks' fish-pond
(*vivarium*)

St Benedict was a practical man, with a considerable knowledge of the problems involved in monastic life, and he knew well the various rules of the monasteries in both the East and West. He held in particular esteem the rules of St Basil and of Cassian. Out of these diverse rules and on the strength of his own experience, he wrote a Rule for the monks of Monte Cassino. In his lifetime, this Rule was also observed at Terracina, a dependency of Monte Cassino, and probably at Subiaco; it also had some influence on the Rule in far-off Vivarium in Calabria, where a monastery was founded by Cassiodorus in 540.

What immediately strikes a modern reader of the Benedictine *Regula* is its common sense and humanity. It deals with spiritual and practical matters such as the duties and obligations of an abbot, who should combine gentleness with severity, the virtues required of a monk, the timetable for everyday life, the discipline, the food, the clothing and numerous other subjects.

The main object of monastic life is the *Opus Dei*, the common daily services chanted in choir. These differ slightly during winter, taking into account the shorter hours of daylight, and are longer and more solemn on Sundays and feast-days. The content of all offices is described in some detail, starting with the night Vigils. The working day is punctuated by seven common prayers: Lauds, Prime, Tierce, Sext, None, Vespers and Compline. Two meals a day, each consisting of two dishes and a pound of bread, are recommended, as well as a pint of wine. Meals, eaten in silence, are to be accompanied by reading by one of the monks. No meat is allowed, except for the sick. The monks are to sleep fully clothed and girded in separate beds in a dormitory lit by candles. Between offices, the monks are to read or to work in the fields, and should there be craftsmen among them, they should work at their crafts, if the abbot allows this. But they should do it with humility and without boastfulness.

St Benedict wrote the Rule during a period of almost incessant wars, invasions, massacres, pestilence and famine. Rome was constantly besieged and changing hands and was, consequently, depopulated. The mode of life offered by St Benedict to his monks must have appeared, against this background, as a haven of peace, stability and orderliness.

The immediate future, however, looked dark. In 577, Monte

9 A dove perched on his shoulder was said to have transmitted the divine voice to St Gregory the Great when he wrote his *Commentaries*. In this ninth- or tenth-century ivory, he sits in a beautifully schematized study with looped curtains, an ornate writing-desk and a chair like an antique capital

Cassino was completely destroyed by the Lombards and was not rebuilt until 720, only to be destroyed again by the Norman conquerors of south Italy in 1046. Rebuilt by the celebrated Abbot Desiderius (1058–87) and altered on a number of subsequent occasions, it was once again reduced to ashes in the last war, to be yet again reconstructed.

6, 7

The Rule of St Benedict, however, proved to be more lasting than the buildings in which it was conceived. Because of its great qualities, because it was so well suited to the mentality and the spiritual needs of the times, it was subsequently adopted throughout Western Europe. The turning-point in the history of Benedictine monasticism was the activity of Gregory the Great. A fervent admirer of St Benedict, he founded the Benedictine monastery of St Andrew on the Coelian in Rome and joined it as a monk, becoming its abbot before being elected to the papacy. In addition, he founded six monasteries in Sicily and supported the spread of the Rule elsewhere. The greatest impetus for the speedy development of the Order was the mission of Benedictine monks, under the leadership of St Augustine, which Gregory sent to England in 596.

9

Celtic monasteries and missions

When the Benedictine monks arrived in England to convert the Anglo-Saxons, the old Celtic Christianity, which had existed in the British Isles before the Germanic invasions, was reduced to small territorial pockets in the west and north. Some British Christians had taken refuge in Brittany and even Spain. In Scotland the southern Picts, converted early in the fifth century by St Ninian from his monastery known as Candida Casa at Whithorn, had by the seventh century reverted to paganism. Only the Welsh, the Cornish and the Irish Churches continued their existence, in isolation from Rome and the developments on the Continent. These Churches were largely monastic, based on the austere example of the 'Desert Fathers' of Egypt. One of the earliest (*c.* 500) of Welsh monasteries was at Llanilltud (probably the present Llantwit Major in Glamorganshire), founded by Illtud, a great 'Teacher of the Britons'. David, regarded as the patron saint of Wales, who founded the monastery at Menevia (St David's), was said to have received his early training at Llanilltud.

10 The early monastic site on the island of Skellig Michael, off the Atlantic coast of Ireland: domical huts built of dry stone, without mortar, cluster near two now-ruined chapels

The Irish Church was, like the Welsh, not episcopal but predominantly monastic, the abbots playing a leading role in Church organization. The monastic schools, which sprang up during the sixth century, were practically the only places in Western Europe where the classics were studied and the tradition of Latin culture preserved and handed down to future generations. In the next century, many foreigners went there for instruction. Scholarship was of little interest to St Benedict and the early Benedictines, and it was under the influence of Irish monks that English and later Continental Benedictine monasticism acquired a love of study and teaching.

These early monasteries, whether in Wales, Cornwall or Scotland (where a monk-missionary, St Mungo or Kentigern, preached at the turn of the sixth and seventh centuries and founded Glasgow), because of the spirit of austerity and deprivation which inspired them, were housed in simple, dry-built buildings and even caves (as, for instance, at Tintagel in Cornwall). In communities such as these, everything was of a purely utilitarian character and things of beauty would have been regarded as sinful. The Irish monks copied and decorated sacred texts, employed modest sculpture to

enrich gravestones, commissioned metal objects with ornamental enamels and above all, built timber and stone churches and monasteries. These were not elaborate or monumental. One of the best preserved of the early monastic sites is on Skellig Michael (an island in the Atlantic off the Kerry coast), nestling on a narrow platform of rock. Five large beehive-shaped huts surround a chapel in the form of an upturned boat, with another smaller chapel on the edge of the site. All important monasteries were subject to rebuilding and pillage in later times and so the evidence of their original buildings is very scanty. But it appears that many had several small churches of wood or stone standing in cemeteries and encircled by a rather haphazard group of monastic buildings, some circular, often large enough to be divided into two stories by timber floors. A circular wall marked the limits of the monastery and outside it there were usually the dwellings of the secular labourers and craftsmen.

By the middle of the century, the spectacular expansion of Irish monasticism had begun. St Columba's missions in Scotland, and the foundation by him of the monastery of Iona (563), from which he ruled a great number of dependent houses, were the first stage in the growth of missionary activity at that time. At the root of this activity was the urge to seek salvation by abandoning a peaceful life at home, to face the dangers of a sea voyage and of foreign lands, to welcome hunger and privation, while carrying the Gospels to those who were in need of enlightenment.

From Iona, the Columban monks sailed in all directions, establishing dependent houses on the islands and the mainland of Scotland. By the seventh century, they had founded a monastery on the island of Lindisfarne, off the coast of Northumbria, and from there Irish monastic influence with its customs and artistic culture penetrated into northern England.

Even more remarkable were the missions of St Columbanus, a monk of Bangor in Co. Down who, in about 590, left Ireland with twelve companions and, in the course of the next twenty-five years, lived in Gaul and Italy, exercising a profound influence on religious life and, to a certain extent, on the civilization of Western Europe. The abbeys of Luxeuil in the Vosges and Bobbio in the Apennines were founded by him and were flourishing centres of religious life and of learning, for some time preserving Celtic observances. The

11 The swirling stylization of Celtic art appears in this Crucifixion scene from an Irish Gospel book, preserved in the abbey of St Gall in Switzerland since the eighth century

influence of Columbanus in Gaul was widespread and many monasteries adopted Celtic customs. The Irish monks, with their tradition of learning, established large libraries and encouraged the copying and decorating of books. A very large number of manuscripts from Bobbio still survive, and the earliest among them exhibit a curious mixture of Celtic and Italian elements of decoration.

Irish missionary activity also left an imprint on Switzerland, for one of the companions of St Columbanus, St Gall, remained there till his death. The celebrated abbey of St Gall which arose over his tomb preserves to this day one of the richest of monastic libraries, and some of the books are of obvious Irish origin.

11

The Celtic monastic missions rendered a valuable service to civilization by bringing Christianity and learning to large parts of Britain and strong moral values to Continental Europe, at a time when they were threatened with extinction. From the artistic point of view, their activities were also of considerable importance, for they introduced Celtic elements into early medieval art.

A few years after St Columbanus travelled from Ireland to Gaul, unaware of the existence of the Benedictine Rule, the forty monks sent from Rome by Gregory the Great landed in Kent in 597, and began their mission of converting the Anglo-Saxons. Within a few years their leader St Augustine, now an archbishop, had founded at Canterbury the first Benedictine monastery outside Italy, that of St Peter and St Paul, later known as St Augustine's.

The plan of this church was not of the basilican type, as might have been expected from Roman monks. A short nave, preceded by a narthex and ending in an apse, was flanked on either side by *porticus* or chapels, containing tombs. One of these chapels was reserved for the tombs of St Augustine and his successors, another for the tombs of King Ethelbert and his wife Bertha. Built of re-used Roman brick, the church presents certain similarities with Early Christian buildings in North Africa and Syria. Churches built on a similar plan in Kent and Essex and associated with St Augustine's missions testify to the high skill of the seventh-century masons, brought no doubt from the Continent, and this type of church persisted with some modifications for many centuries in Anglo-Saxon England.

In sculpture also, the standards achieved are surprising in their technical ability and beauty. The fragments of the high cross from Reculver Minster in Kent bear the striking imprint of Mediterranean art of the Early Christian period, but they are incomparably finer than anything that contemporary artists on the Continent were producing.

Needless to say, St Augustine's mission brought from Rome liturgical books, vestments, vessels, relics and all kinds of objects necessary for their missionary work, and Pope Gregory and his successors sent more in due course. One such Gospel Book, which belonged to St Augustine's Abbey at Canterbury, is still preserved (Cambridge, Corpus Christi College, MS 286). According to the Benedictine Rule, much time in monastic life was devoted to reading; no less than two hours daily were set aside for this activity. Thus, the need for a large number of books was great, and for this reason, from very early times, monks copied books and often decorated them. The lavishly illuminated *Codex Aureus* (Stock-

13

15

12 The Benedictine monks of Christchurch, Canterbury, portray themselves doing homage to St Benedict, 'father of monks and leader' (early eleventh century)

13, 14, 15 Classical-inspired motifs and Barbaric interlace are combined in a fragment of the high cross from Reculver (*left*) and in manuscripts copied at Canterbury in the eighth century. *Right:* David harping, from a Psalter. In the *Codex Aureus* (*far right*), St Matthew sits on a throne with an intricate knot pattern

holm, Royal Library) is such a copy, made at Canterbury in the eighth century from a sixth-century Italian original. Copies were not always faithful to the model and an eighth-century Psalter from St Augustine's, Canterbury (British Museum, MS Cotton Vespasian A. I), incorporates figure subjects derived from a Greek model with ornamentation of Hiberno-Saxon inspiration. Further objects for liturgical use and books must have reached Canterbury when, in 669, Theodore of Tarsus, a Greek educated in Tarsus and in Athens, was appointed archbishop of Canterbury. Two years later, his friend Hadrian, an African by birth, and abbot of a monastery near Naples, 'a great scholar in Greek and Latin', as Bede calls him, became abbot of St Augustine's. Thus England became a great repository of ancient texts, religious and secular, many no doubt illuminated, and these exercised a considerable influence on the learning and the arts of Anglo-Saxon England for many centuries to come.

The missions led from Canterbury met with steady success in the southern part of the country, but the north and the midlands, on the other hand, were converted by the Celtic missionaries from

14

26

Lindisfarne. By the middle of the seventh century when, with the exception of Sussex, the whole country was at least nominally Christian, the matter of the different Celtic and Roman customs became pressing. The differences between the Celtic and Roman liturgies, between the systems of calculating the date of Easter, between the shapes of the tonsure, one shaved across the head from ear to ear, the other circular in imitation of Christ's Crown of Thorns, could not exist side by side indefinitely. Moreover, the consecration of bishops by the Celtic Church was sometimes regarded by the Roman party as uncanonical. In the end, the Roman customs prevailed and, though the Irish Church continued in its old traditions for a long time, they were eventually abandoned. After the Synod of Whitby of 664 the Celtic monasteries of Northumbria adopted the Roman customs, and gradually the great monasteries founded by the Irish missionaries, as for instance Lindisfarne, became Benedictine.

The man who was an enthusiastic supporter of Benedictine monasticism was St Benedict Biscop (d. 689). For three years, he was a monk at Lérins in Provence, then for a time was abbot of St

Augustine's Abbey at Canterbury. He founded two monasteries in his native Northumbria, St Peter at Wearmouth (674) and St Paul at Jarrow (681). It was in the latter that the Venerable Bede (d. 735) spent most of his life as a monk, writing his religious and historical works.

Another great supporter of Benedictine monasticism was St Wilfrid, formerly a monk of Lindisfarne. He introduced the Roman customs into the Celtic monasteries at Ripon and York and into a monastery which he founded at Hexham.

Both Biscop and Wilfrid made several journeys to Rome and Gaul, and brought back with them craftsmen and works of art. Biscop procured the services of John, the arch-cantor of St Peter's in Rome, who came to Northumbria for a year to teach the monks 'the theory and practice of singing and reading aloud' (Bede). The second half of the seventh century and the whole of the eighth century were a Golden Age of religious life and of learning centred on Benedictine monasteries in the north of England. During this time, the arts of every kind also flourished with an intensity which earned that period the name of 'Northumbrian Renaissance'.

In about 700 there were over fifty stone churches in England, and a few still survive, even if only in a fragmentary state. The crypts of Ripon and Hexham are of that time. In Northumbria alone, some thirty monastic houses existed and, although much building was made in wood, stone architecture, often of a very ambitious type, was firmly established for major monasteries. Stone sculpture was used extensively to decorate buildings (frieze at Hexham) and furnishings (bench ends at Monkwearmouth) and, above all, for high crosses, a peculiarity of the British Isles. In 675, Benedict Biscop brought from Gaul craftsmen to teach the English how to make glass, so necessary in monasteries in the northern climate. Fragments of coloured glass from windows were found recently in excavations at Jarrow and Monkwearmouth.

The copying and decorating of manuscripts, this monastic occupation *par excellence*, resulted in some remarkable examples from this period in Northumbria. As at Canterbury, a great number of books were brought to the northern monasteries from the Continent. One such manuscript was the mid-sixth-century *Codex Grandior*, the Vulgate Bible, which came from the famous library of Cassiodorus in his Calabrian monastery at Vivarium.

17

16
18

16, 17, 18 *Above*: a carved animal appears on a bench-end from Monkwearmouth. *Below*: the crypt at Hexham, of *c.* 672.
Right: the shaft of the Bewcastle cross

19, 20 Cassiodorus in his study, with book-cupboard and writing tools, served as model for the prophet Ezra in a mid-sixth-century Italian manuscript. A faithful English copy, made over a century later, is the *Codex Amiatinus* (*right*). The contemporary English artist of the *Lindisfarne Gospels* transformed Ezra into the Evangelist Matthew (*left*), flattening the figure and eliminating the setting

This important book, together with others from the same source, was obtained by St Ceolfrith, joint abbot of Wearmouth and Jarrow, and teacher of Bede, when he was in Rome in 678. Three copies of the *Codex Grandior* were made in Northumbria during the last decade of the seventh century, one for each of the monasteries and a third to be taken by Ceolfrith on his journey to Rome to be presented to the Pope. This last still survives, having been given, at a later date, to the Benedictine abbey of S. Salvatore on the slopes of Monte Amiata, south of Siena. Known as *Codex Amiatinus*, it is now in the Laurentian Library in Florence. This gigantic book of over two thousand pages, each covered with two columns of beautiful script, has a few illuminations, including a full-page representation of Cassiodorus, seated in his study at Vivarium, disguised as the prophet Ezra. This page shows at once to what extent the painting at Vivarium preserved the classical tradition of naturalism, and also with what competence the English monks were able to copy such unfamiliar models, so different from the native artistic traditions. The cupboard with books, the furniture of the study, the tools for writing and illuminating books scattered about, all these give unique information about a monastic scriptorium of that early age.

Not all copies were as faithful to their models as the *Codex Amiatinus*. An almost contemporary book, written by Eadfrith between 698 and 721 at Lindisfarne, and known as the Lindisfarne Gospels (British Museum, MS Cotton Nero D. IV), includes a miniature also copied from the *Codex Grandior*, but this time the copyist did not want, or was unable, to follow the naturalism of the

19 original picture and made it more two-dimensional and ornamental. Even more striking are the purely decorative pages of this book, based on native Hiberno-Saxon art, best known in metalwork, but which had already been, in about the year 675, adopted

21 for book illumination in the Book of Durrow (Dublin, Trinity College, MS 57), probably also a Northumbrian work.

21 Interlace border from the Book of Durrow, *c.* 675

The old missionary spirit, so characteristic of Irish monasticism, was not yet dead, and it affected Northumbria during this period of its 'Renaissance' as well as other Anglo-Saxon kingdoms. The 'Apostle of Frisia', St Willibrord (658–739), was a pupil of the monks of Ripon, and spent twelve years in the Irish monastery of Rathmelsigi. The famous Benedictine monastery at Echternach, near Trier, founded by him in 698, was clearly at first populated by English and Irish monks, for the painted pages of the Echternach Gospels (Paris, Bibliothèque Nationale, MS lat. 9389), made during his lifetime, are superb examples of the Hiberno–Saxon style transplanted to the Continent.

22 The 'Apostle of Germany', St Boniface (680–754), the missionary and organizer of the Church in Germany and founder of the monastery at Fulda, was a native of Crediton in Devon. Most

22 St Boniface administering baptism: detail of a miniature from the eleventh-century Sacramentary of Fulda

of his followers were his countrymen and included St Lul (d. 786), a monk of Malmesbury and founder of the abbey of Hersfeld, and St Willibald (d. 786), an English monk who, on his way back from the East, settled for ten years at Monte Cassino (730–40) and helped in re-establishing the monastery there before joining St Boniface in Germany. He founded the double house for monks and nuns at Heidenheim in Württemberg where his brother, St Winnebald, and his sister St Walburga succeeded each other as abbot and abbess.

The conversion of Germany by monastic missionaries, chiefly from England, extended Benedictine monasticism to vast new territories. During the same period, monasticism was expanding in Gaul and the Columban customs were being rapidly replaced by the Benedictine Rule. But at the same time as the monasticism of the West was gaining unprecedented prestige and developing rapidly, there appeared signs of serious difficulties, which ultimately brought it into disrepute and decline, if only temporarily.

The reason for the decline, paradoxically, was the very multiplication and prosperity of the monasteries. Although the monks were forbidden by the Rule to possess any private property, the monastery as a community was frequently very rich because of endowments, gifts and its own good management. Many monasteries were founded by kings, powerful nobles, bishops, and in time, these felt entitled to treat their foundations as their private property (*Eigenklöster* as they are called in scholarly literature). They appointed stooges as abbots, frequently their relatives, to foster their own interests. The decline of the monastic spirit and discipline was, in such circumstances, understandable.

33

The Carolingian reforms

The policy of Charlemagne aimed at the *renovatio imperii romani*, by which was meant chiefly the revival of the Christian Empire, the Empire as it existed under Constantine the Great (d. 337). This Carolingian revival embraced all forms of secular and religious life including, naturally, the monasteries. Although Charles entrusted the revival of teaching and learning to scholars, who were not necessarily monks or clerics, a number of his closest associates were monks, or were, in one way or another, connected with monasteries. Alcuin, the intellectual architect of the Carolingian Renaissance, was a scholar of the cathedral school at York; but, towards the end of his life, he became abbot of Tours (796), and established a famous library and school there. Einhard, the historian, was brought up in the monastery of Fulda. The theologian and poet Theodulf was made abbot of Fleury. Charles's determination to improve education in his domains can be seen in his numerous capitularies, ordering the formation of schools in every bishop's house and in every monastery. Some of the monastic schools became famous centres of learning, for example Tours,

23, 24 The ideal layout of a monastery about 820 appears in the St Gall plan (*far right*), redrawn so that its parts can be more easily seen. The reconstruction (*right*, looking from bottom left in the plan), shows how the complex might have looked, clustered around the church with its two apses and western towers. The general disposition changed little over the centuries (see, for instance, Ills. 6, 50, 54, 62)

Fulda, Corbie, Centula (St Riquier) and St Gall. Charlemagne was also anxious for monasteries to follow the rules correctly, and he obtained from Monte Cassino a copy of what was believed to be the original version of the Rule of St Benedict.

During the reign of Charles's son, Louis the Pious, monastic reform was carried out under the emperor's auspices by St Benedict of Aniane (c. 750–821). Benedict was a soldier who turned monk, and devoted his life to reforming monastic life in the Empire. He founded a monastic house on his estate at Aniane in Languedoc and, though at first he thought the Benedictine Rule not austere enough, he eventually adopted it and for the rest of his life was its fervent supporter. He was called to numerous monasteries to reform the discipline, and these activities brought him into contact with King Louis of Aquitaine, the future emperor. Louis, on his accession, put him in charge of all monasteries in the Empire and built for him a monastery, called Inde (later Cornelimünster), close to Aachen, which was to be an example to all the other monasteries. At a meeting of all abbots from the Empire at Aachen in 817, the Rule of St Benedict was modified, taking into account past experience, and it was decreed that it should be observed by all monasteries.

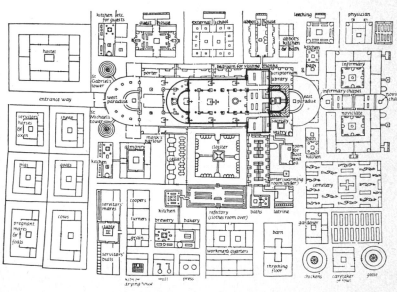

Amongst the important changes in the original Rule were those which concerned work in the fields, no longer required of monks, the prohibition of teaching except of oblates (or children destined by their parents to become monks), and changes in the daily liturgy. This last was the result of the other two. The monk of St Benedict's day divided his time between prayer and work, but now physical work was no longer obligatory and the *Opus Dei* had become much longer and more elaborate. This 'ritualistic movement' was to gain in strength in the future, especially in the Cluniac Order. In St Benedict's time, a monastery had only a small number of monks who were priests. But as time went on, the Mass was celebrated not only on Sundays but every day, and as the services became more elaborate, so consequently the number of priests in a monastery increased. The reform of St Benedict of Aniane gave this trend a further impetus and, in time, most monks were priests.

The abbey of Inde became the centre for the training of monks in the modified rule, each monastery being obliged by the emperor to send one or two monks there to familiarize themselves with the customs of this *schola monachorum*. It is in the light of this attempt at uniformity in monastic practice that one should view the celebrated plan preserved in the library of the abbey of St Gall, made *23, 24* in about 820, shortly after the Synod of Aachen. The plan was intended as an ideal for future Benedictine abbeys, and was devised in the circle of Benedict of Aniane. The abbey church was to have two apses, at the east and the west, following roughly the precedent of Fulda, newly rebuilt. Adjoining the church, on its south side, is the cloister, with the monks' buildings on its three sides. There is no chapter-house as yet, for the monks used the church for their meetings. The dormitory, on the east side of the cloister, adjoins the south transept and is linked with it by a passage. To the east of the church is the hospital with its separate chapel and the novitiate. Other buildings, such as the abbot's house, the guest house, the servants' quarters, the stables, etc., are placed sensibly within a rectangular layout.

As the St Gall plan is instructive on points connected with the general arrangement of a Carolingian monastery, two seventeenth-century engravings based on an eleventh-century miniature show vividly what the elevation of the famous monastery of Centula *25* (St Riquier) in Picardy looked like. Built between 790 and 799 by

Angilbert, the learned friend of Charlemagne, on a basilican plan, it had two axial towers and an atrium with more towers. The façade block or 'westwork' was, according to Conant, 'the earliest really imposing and boldly articulated façade in church architecture – a historical landmark'. The western block motif was repeated at Rheims and at Corbie, and again in Corbie's dependency at Corvey on the Weser (Nova Corbeia, founded in 822), and became a 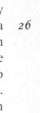 favourite feature of Ottonian and Romanesque church building in Germany. Corvey was the base for missionary work among the heathen Saxons, and it was also from there that St Anskar went to Denmark and Sweden before becoming the archbishop of Bremen. Although his missions were a partial success, the Scandinavian countries were not converted till much later.

26

25, 26 The eighth-century abbey of Centula (*above*), had a church with two towered transepts and a westwork. A westwork of 873–85 survives, somewhat heightened, at Corvey (*right*)

The break-up of the Carolingian Empire led to a period of political and economic anarchy. The repeated invasions of the Northmen, the Hungarians and the Moors, the savage and ruthless behaviour of rulers and the wretchedness of everyday existence were hardly conditions in which the contemplative life could flourish. Monasteries were sacked and burnt; monks often became fugitives, concerned only to save their lives, their few possessions and their sacred relics. In such circumstances, it was difficult, even impossible, to observe the monastic rule. The complaint of King Alfred (reigned 871–99), that at the beginning of his reign nobody in the south of England knew Latin, was symptomatic of the state of affairs in Europe; though admittedly, because of the Viking raids, Britain declined sooner and more drastically than the Empire. That monastic life, and with it Europe's civilization, was saved from complete disintegration was due to a few men of great faith and courage, who set themselves the task of restoring moral values by first reforming the monasteries.

The work before them was enormous and not without personal danger. Raffredus, abbot of Farfa in Lazio, was poisoned in 936 by two of his monks because he attempted to enforce the Benedictine Rule there. One of his murderers, Campo, became abbot and he and his accomplice lived in the monastery with their wives and children. Another attempt at reform resulted in the expulsion of Campo from the monastery, but the new abbot was also poisoned. Not until the end of the century was Farfa successfully reformed by an abbot who, however, in order to carry out this task, had to use simony to be elected.

One of the most famous monasteries in Gaul was Fleury (now St Benoît-sur-Loire), owing its great reputation to the relics of St Benedict, which the monks of Fleury claimed to have rescued from Monte Cassino. Even this monastery was in need of reform, and when in the tenth century Odo, abbot of Cluny, went there in order to enforce the Rule, he was met by armed monks ready to resist the unwanted interference. It is a measure of Odo's courage and saintliness that in an age when only brute force was understood, he gained entry, as testified by his contemporary and biographer, John of Salerno, with the disarming words: 'I come peacefully –

27 The porch of St Benoît-sur-Loire – Fleury – seen from the north, showing eleventh-century capitals and sections of decorative frieze

to hurt no one, injure no one, but that I may correct those who are not living according to Rule.'

The reform of the monastic Rule at Farfa and at Fleury was due *27* to the activities of Cluny, the monastery to which European civilization owes an enormous debt.

This Burgundian monastery, founded in 910 by William the Pious, duke of Aquitaine, was placed under the direct control of Rome, and thus it was exempted from any future local interference. This, combined with a series of exceptionally wise, energetic and saintly abbots, assured Cluny's importance. The early abbots devoted themselves to reform, and this they carried out not only in France but also in the Empire, Italy, Spain and England. Though at first the reformed abbeys retained their autonomy, gradually a close link was established between them and Cluny. The virtual

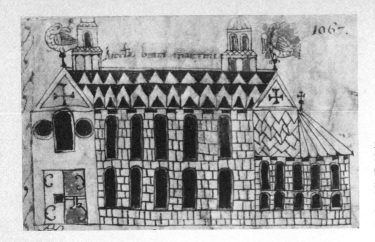

28 The church of St Martin-des-Champs, in Paris, as it appears at the beginning of the Cluniac abbey's Chronicle

independence of each Benedictine abbey was replaced by an organization of a feudal character. It was in this way that the Cluniac Order was born and, during the abbacy of St Hugh (1049–1109), granted official recognition by Pope Urban II. By then a number of important abbeys belonged to the Cluniac Order – La Charité-sur-Loire, Moissac, St Martial at Limoges, St Martin-des-Champs in Paris, and also the first nunnery, Marcigny in Burgundy, which was founded in 1056.

28

The Cluniac Order was essentially aristocratic, since the monks came chiefly from the nobility. Manual work was no longer considered a suitable occupation for monks, most of whom were priests, and was replaced by an elaborate liturgy, which took up most of their time. Work in the fields and in the workshops was entrusted to lay brothers. Cluny's organization was based on the feudal idea of hierarchy. The abbot of Cluny was an absolute ruler, who often nominated his own successor. All Cluniac monasteries were subject to him and they were not allowed the status of abbeys, but were called priories. Only a few very ancient foundations, reformed by Cluny, were allowed to retain their former title. Not all priories were equal. As in contemporary society where the king was at the apex, with barons, knights, lesser nobility and the rest in a descending scale of importance, so was the abbot of the Cluniac Order the head of the whole hierarchy of subordinate members. The five privileged priories, known as the five daughters of Cluny, including Lewes, the mother-house of the English Cluniacs, had dependencies of their own. The abbot appointed the priors, but the priors of the five privileged priories appointed the priors of their dependencies. The link with Cluny was close, and every monk had to come to Cluny at least once in his lifetime, for all novices had to be admitted to the Order at Cluny.

The Cluniac Order expanded with a phenomenal speed from the middle of the tenth century onwards and, at the height of its popularity, early in the twelfth century, it consisted of nearly fifteen hundred monasteries. The popes were great champions of the Order and several of them were formerly Cluniac monks. The secular clergy were, generally speaking, less well disposed to Cluny, and some bishops particularly resented its exemption from their control. One extreme case is that of Adalberon, bishop of Laon (d. 1030), who gave expression to his disapproval of Cluny in a satirical poem, in which he ridiculed Cluniac customs.

There can be no doubt that these customs were excessively ritualistic. Even St Peter Damian (d. 1072), a severe reformer, who greatly admired Cluny, found the Cluniac timetable too full and exacting. In fact, this excess of ceremonial is considered to be the main reason for the decline of the Cluniacs in the latter half of the twelfth century. However, this decline followed two hundred years of expansion, and the achievements of the Order during that time were truly remarkable.

As well as reforming specific abbeys, the Cluniacs also inspired – sometimes indirectly – reforms in a number of countries. The English reform of the tenth century was short-lived, but it produced an extraordinary blossoming of religious life and the arts. This reform was due to St Dunstan, St Oswald and St Ethelwold. The first was monk and abbot at Glastonbury and subsequently archbishop of Canterbury, the second was ordained at Fleury, became bishop of Worcester and then archbishop of York, and the third was a monk at Glastonbury, then abbot of Abingdon and finally bishop of Winchester. These men were in touch with the reform movement in Flanders and at Fleury, and revived monastic life in many ancient foundations dispersed by Viking invasions. The outcome of their efforts was the code approved by the Synod of Winchester (c. 970), known as the *Regularis Concordia*, which followed the tradition of monasticism as modified by Benedict of Aniane, but with many innovations peculiar to England. In the second half of the tenth century, over thirty monasteries for men and six or more for women were thriving and, in them, all forms of intellectual and artistic life. Buildings were repaired or erected *30* afresh. The so-called 'Winchester School' of illumination, practised in all southern monasteries, ivory carving, metalwork, stone sculpture and other arts, received a great stimulus. At this time English works of art, especially illuminated books, reached various Continental monastic centres, for instance Fleury, and became a source of inspiration for local development. The most striking example of this was the abbey of St Bertin where, under Abbot Odbert (986–1004), who was a painter himself, the Winchester School style was absorbed and modified to produce works of a *29* hybrid kind.

The renewed Danish invasions of England, and political conditions during the first half of the eleventh century, led to a decline in monastic discipline, and it was not until after the Norman Conquest that the reform of monasteries was carried out on a vast scale, leading to the period of their greatest development and prestige.

More lasting than the tenth-century reform of the Anglo-Saxon monasteries was the reform carried out in Flanders and Lotharingia. The Lotharingian movement, which was independent of Cluny, started at Gorzé, near Metz, and led initially to the reform of some seventy abbeys.

Among the great reformers of the age, the man who stands out most particularly, because of his extraordinary achievement, is William of Volpiano. This monk from Piedmont, who followed Abbot Mayeul to Cluny, became abbot of St Bénigne at Dijon, founded the abbey of Fruttuaria near Volpiano, reformed Fécamp and a string of other abbeys in Normandy, and before his death ruled over twelve hundred monks in forty abbeys. It is not surprising, therefore, to find close artistic connections between Normandy and Burgundy, a striking example being the architectural sculpture of Bernay Abbey (second quarter of the eleventh century) which is derived, at least in part, from that of St Bénigne *38* at Dijon (early eleventh century). The Norman reform resulted in an extraordinary flowering of intellectual life based on such monasteries as Bec, when Lanfranc was the head of the school. In artistic matters also, and especially in architecture and manuscript painting, Normandy became one of the most progressive and inventive regions in eleventh-century Europe.

42

29, 30 Fluttering drapery and lush foliage characterize such 'Winchester School' manuscripts as the Benedictional of Ethelwold, of 975–80 (*right*). The linear drapery reappears in a miniature by Odbert of St Bertin (detail *below*)

   The energetic reform of English monasticism after the Norman Conquest was carried out by Lanfranc, who had been elevated to the archbishopric of Canterbury. His *Consuetudines*, or 'Customary' for his monks of Christchurch, Canterbury, is not unnaturally based on the customs practised at Bec, and it was adopted by a number of English monasteries. The appointment of Norman abbots to English houses, and the influx of monks from across the Channel, ensured the thoroughness of the reform and, as a side-effect, this had a most profound effect on artistic life. It is no exaggeration to say that, as a result of the Norman Conquest, England was invaded by Romanesque art in its Norman form, chiefly through monastic channels.

43

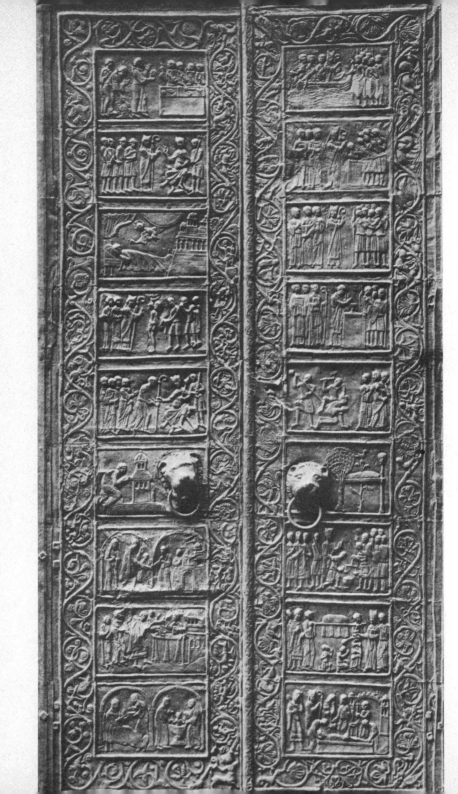

Chapter Two

To the Limits of Christendom

The Cluniac reform also spread to Rome and other Italian centres, but did not take lasting root there. Italy, with its extraordinary mingling of races and cultures, had some monasteries of an unusual character. For instance, the famous abbey of St Boniface and St Alexis, on the Aventine in Rome, was founded for both Greek and Latin communities. From this house many missionaries went to eastern Europe, and it was here that St Adalbert of Prague was a monk before his martyrdom while converting the Prussians (997). His life and martyrdom are immortalized in many scenes depicted on the bronze doors of Gniezno Cathedral, where his body was buried.   *31*

In those parts of Italy where Byzantine rule or influence persisted, Basilian monasteries continued to exist side by side with Latin, at least until the middle of the thirteenth century.

The Normans who, in the course of the eleventh century, conquered southern Italy and Sicily, were not supporters of Cluny, and only one Cluniac priory, at Sciacca in Sicily, existed in their dominions. However, an order which imitated the Cluniac customs was established at Cava dei Tirreni near Salerno. This   *32* *Ordo Cavensis* ruled over forty abbeys, thirty-five priories and sixty churches, with a monastic community of three thousand. Among the monasteries of the Order were the celebrated S. Paolo fuori le mura in Rome and Monreale, the foundation of King William II, as well as a number of Greek monasteries in Calabria, such as Rossano. The Order established a foothold in the Holy Land in 1070, founding S. Maria Latina with the hospital of St John at Jerusalem.

The *Ordo Cavensis*, supported by the Norman rulers, dominated Sicily and the south, while the region north of Naples and up to Rome was under the influence of Monte Cassino. Restored in the tenth century on the model of Cluny, this cradle of Western monasticism became a flourishing centre of religious and artistic

31 The exploits of St Adalbert are celebrated on the bronze doors of Gniezno Cathedral in Poland, *c.* 1170. His martyrdom is shown above the right-hand knocker, his burial at the bottom

life. Favoured by the popes and the emperors, it grew in power, wealth and influence. Odo of Cluny visited Monte Cassino in 940 and established cordial relations, which were to last throughout the period of Cluny's greatness.

The reform movement started by Cluny was gathering momentum and, in the eleventh century, it embraced the whole of Western Europe. In no other country outside France was the Cluniac influence stronger than in Spain. Little is known of early Spanish monasticism which, because of the Arab Conquest of 711, developed largely independently of that in Gaul and Italy. Its peculiar customs, known as 'Mozarabic', were cultivated not only in the monasteries in the Arab-held territories, but also in the Christian north. Only in the Spanish March, under Frankish domination, was the Benedictine Rule practised, in such monasteries as Ripoll and Leyre. During the eleventh century some of the most important Spanish abbeys became Cluniac, and many new ones were

33 founded as Cluniac priories. S. Juan de la Peña became Cluniac in 1022, and was followed by S. Millan de la Cogolla, Leyre and Sahagun. Silos and Ripoll adopted Cluniac customs without, however, joining the Order.

32, 33 The Cluniac Order was imitated in Italy at Cava dei Tirreni: its eleventh-century cloister (*below*), built up against the rock, incorporates Roman columns. S. Juan de la Peña (*opposite*) became Cluniac in 1022: the west end of the upper church, consecrated in 1095, and the west range of the cloister emerge from an overhanging cliff

Of all the monarchs of the age, Alfonso VI (d. 1109) was the most enthusiastic admirer of Cluny, and the greatest benefactor of this Burgundian abbey. It was during his rule, and under the influence of St Hugh of Cluny, that the ancient Mozarabic Rite was replaced by the Roman in his realm.

The reform movement in the Empire was, at least in part, due to the activities of such abbeys as Gorzé, or Brogne and others in Flanders. In addition, the Cluniac reform came by various routes. The direct influence was seen in the group of monasteries headed by Hirsau, but the Cluniac customs also reached Germany by way of Italy, from Fruttuaria. The emperors, especially the Ottos and Henry II, were great supporters of reform, not only of monasticism

47

but also of all forms of religious life, but when the quarrel with the papacy developed over the question of the investiture, Henry IV adopted an attitude of open hostility towards the monasteries.

In the countries newly converted to Christianity the work of the monasteries was of the greatest importance. In fact, the conversion of the Scandinavian countries was due to monastic missionaries from Germany and England. In spite of the early successes of Slav missions among the Czechs and Poles, it was Rome that finally succeeded in converting them. The first Benedictine monasteries in Bohemia date from the end of the tenth century. Those in Poland were swept away by the pagan reaction of 1034, and only from the middle of the eleventh century onwards did well-endowed monasteries begin to appear in large numbers. Tyniec, near Cracow, where recent excavations have revealed the foundations of the church and the well-preserved tombs of some of the abbots, is one of the oldest.

King Stephen of Hungary was in contact with Cluny and the reforming centres in Lotharingia, for he was a warm supporter of monks and monasteries. Monasteries were the essential means of bringing to the newly converted countries not only Christianity, but also learning and various crafts and skills.

Romanesque art was born in monasteries. The earliest architectural experiments, which are known by the convenient label of First Romanesque, were conducted chiefly in Benedictine monasteries in northern Italy. These buildings, often quite crude, were built not by monks but by secular masons, the *magistri comacini*, who were organized in guilds, and carried on their profession throughout the darkest period of the Middle Ages. S. Pietro at Agliate (*c.* 875) and S. Pietro at Civate (*c.* 1040) are examples of the early and late development of this First Romanesque style. The abbey of Civate, built on a high mountain peak in an ideally defensible and secluded position, is an ambitious structure with two apses and a crypt, and is decorated with stucco reliefs and wall-paintings.

    The First Romanesque style spread east to Dalmatia and west to France, and even further to Catalonia where, in contact with

34
35

34, 35 *Opposite:* S. Pietro at Agliate, showing the apse of *c.* 875 and the baptistery of *c.* 900 (left foreground), both built of strong, rough masonry. *Below:* the crypt at Civate is decorated with stucco, including a now damaged Crucifixion behind the altar

36 *Left:* the tunnel-vaulted nave of S. Pedro de Roda, of *c.* 1022, looking east

37 *Below:* the marble lintel of St Genis-des-Fontaines, one of the earliest medieval portal enrichments, dated by an inscription to 1020–21

Mozarabic architecture, great innovations were made, especially in improving the vaulting of churches. These vital experiments were carried out in Benedictine monasteries, of which St Martin-du-Canigou, S. Maria de Ripoll, St Michel-de-Cuxa, S. Vicente de Cardona and S. Pedro de Roda are a few of the most famous.

36   It was also in the part-Spanish, part-French region of Roussillon and in Catalonia that the first ambitious attempts at monumental sculpture in marble were made. The lintel of St Genis-des-Fontaines (1020–21) and related sculpture in the nearby monasteries,

37 though modest in every way, together form an important landmark in the history of sculpture. After many centuries of neglect, architectural sculpture once more gained recognition at St Genis-des-Fontaines, by being placed over the entrance to the church. Here again, as in the case of contemporary buildings, the monks presumably acted as patrons and advisers. Most important, by providing the opportunities, they gave the arts a new and much needed impetus.

38 *Above:* the raised hands of grotesque figures take the place of volutes at the corners of a capital in the crypt of St Bénigne, Dijon

39 *Right:* St Philibert, Tournus, looking from the groin-vaulted aisle up into the transverse tunnel vaults of the nave, separated by arches of ashlar

The First Romanesque style penetrated north along the rivers Rhône and Rhine, and some of the most spectacular buildings of this early age are the abbey churches of St Philibert at Tournus (where many forms of vaulting were experimented with), and *39* St Bénigne at Dijon; the latter was built by William of Volpiano, in the first years of the eleventh century; only the crypt survives, decorated by a series of carved capitals, among the earliest examples *38* of Romanesque sculpture which still survive.

A contemporary architectural development, based on quite different traditions, was taking place in Ottonian Germany. Modelled partly on Early Christian and Carolingian basilicas and influenced by Byzantine structures and their decoration, Ottonian buildings have a monumental character of their own. Their impressive size, the peculiarities of their plans, and the use of towers exceeding in size and number anything elsewhere, put these buildings in a class by themselves. For instance the church of St Michael at Hildesheim, built by Bishop Bernward for the Benedictine monks in the first years of the eleventh century, has two choirs, two transepts and four towers, and is an imposing building which had few rivals in the West at that time.

In 1912, the French art historian Lefèvre-Pontalis introduced the term 'the Benedictine plan', which is used to describe a church with a central apse and a choir flanked by side-aisles terminating in apses; the design included further apses in each arm of the transept and a tower over the crossing, and, usually but not always, two western towers at the beginning of the aisled nave. Although many Benedictine churches are of this type, this plan does not seem to be exclusively Benedictine, nor does it apply, for instance, to such Benedictine churches as Hildesheim.

The 'Benedictine plan' was used in the tenth century (before 981) at Cluny for the building which, because it replaced the original structure, was called by Professor Conant Cluny II. This plan, introduced into Normandy from Burgundy by William of Volpiano, eventually reached England, where it had a great vogue throughout the Romanesque period.

The 'Benedictine plan' of Cluny II was imitated in other countries as well. The most important Romanesque building in Switzerland is Payerne, the church where, at that time, the emperors were crowned as kings of Burgundy.★ Payerne was founded in 967 as a Cluniac priory and was much favoured by Abbot Odilo, under whose patronage the rebuilding was started. It was usual to begin building a church at its east end but in the case of Payerne the work was done piecemeal, in order to preserve the

★ The kingdom of Burgundy, which included Switzerland, the region along the Rhône from Lyons to the sea, and Provence, belonged at that time to the Empire, and should not be confused with the duchy of Burgundy, which owed its allegiance to the French kingdom. Cluny was in the duchy, though practically on its border with the Empire.

40 Interior of the Benedictine church of St Michael at Hildesheim,
looking west from the raised eastern transept. On the left is the great
Romanesque bronze chandelier. The painted ceiling is *c.* 1200

41 *Left*: St Peter, holding his key, appears with Christ in Majesty in this capital from the Cluniac church of Payerne, *c.* 1080

42 *Right*: Charlemagne and his knights ride into battle against the Moors – an image to inspire pilgrims, from the *Codex Callixtinus, c.* 1130

old tenth-century abbey church for services as long as possible. The apse was the last part to be built, about 1080, and incorporates a particularly interesting twin capital showing Christ in Majesty and St Peter on His right. To be properly understood, this composition must be viewed in the context of contemporary events. Abbot Ulric of Payerne (later St Ulric) was deeply involved in the contest of empire and papacy, siding with Pope Gregory against the Emperor Henry IV. In this controversy the arguments of the pope were based on the claim that his power was derived from St Peter. The extraordinary place allocated to St Peter in the apse at Payerne must thus be seen as propaganda for the pope's party.

A plan based on that of Cluny II was adopted by the German abbey of Hirsau and by its dependencies. From 1079, Hirsau followed the Cluniac customs, though in a somewhat modified form, and within less than twenty years it ruled over thirty new monasteries, while more than a hundred old ones adopted the Cluniac customs. The Hirsau Congregation was particularly popular in the south, but the period of expansion and prosperity was short, and during the twelfth century it declined.

The plan of Cluny II is also reflected in some Spanish churches, but unfortunately many important monasteries which adopted Cluniac customs there have been destroyed.

The road to Compostela

While the 'Benedictine plan' was being adopted all over Europe, another spectacular type of monastic church came into being. This was the 'pilgrimage church', of which the most outstanding examples are the abbeys on the route to the most romantic of medieval pilgrimage centres, Santiago de Compostela.

43–45

The claim that the body of St James had been discovered there gradually made Santiago a pilgrimage place of some importance, but it was only in the eleventh century that it acquired international repute and became as important a place of pilgrimage as Rome and Jerusalem. For a long time, scholars claimed that this sudden growth in the popularity of Santiago was the work of Cluny. Cluny was supposed to have encouraged the movement of pilgrims, for, having built a network of Cluniac priories along the route, it was making huge financial profits from this enterprise. The truth is that although Cluny undoubtedly encouraged the pilgrimages to Santiago, as it encouraged pilgrimages to Jerusalem and Rome, it was not responsible for them. The *Codex Callixtinus*, which includes the famous *Pilgrims' Guide*, was not Cluniac-inspired.

42

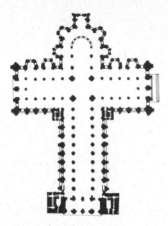

43, 44, 45 At Santiago de
Compostela (*above* and *left*) and
in other churches on the
pilgrimage roads such as Conques
(*opposite*), a continuous aisle runs
round the building, past the shrine
in the choir (at top in the plan).
The churches also have in common
tunnel-vaulted naves and an
elevation of two storeys only,
arcade and gallery

The enormous popularity of Santiago was due not to any
monastic conspiracy, but to the spirit of the age. The *chansons de
geste*, which flourished in the eleventh century on the pilgrimage
routes to Santiago, fired the imagination with stories of heroes,
especially that of Roland.

Roland's valiant exploits and death while fighting the Moors
must have been the inspiration for many pilgrimages to Santiago.
The Moors were still in possession of the greater part of the
Peninsula, as they had been in the time of Charles the Great when
Roland died. Encouraged by the Church, the desire to free Spain

56

46 St James the Slayer of Moors, dressed like a Crusader, appears to awe-struck worshippers on a tympanum at Santiago de Compostela

from the rule of the infidel became the driving force of the pilgrimage movement. A pilgrimage led, in many cases, to the joining of the Crusade against the Arabs. It is no coincidence that the reconquest of Spain was contemporary with the greatest popularity of Santiago. The pilgrimage and the holy war became, in many minds, one and the same thing. The image of St James on a white horse slaying the Moors, appearing miraculously at the battle of Clavijo, became the symbol of both. He is shown as the Moorslayer, the *Matamoros*, on many church tympana, including one at Santiago itself.

The movement of pilgrims meant that not only objects of art and souvenirs travelled long distances, thus spreading artistic styles from country to country, but also that churches had to be built in

42

46

such a manner as to allow the smooth circulation of large crowds of pilgrims. For the pilgrims were not satisfied with simply travelling to Santiago, but visited *en route* many of those churches which were famous for their relics. The *Pilgrims' Guide* lists and describes many such churches which were worthy of a visit. Among them are the Romanesque abbeys of St Martin at Tours, St Martial at Limoges, Ste Foy at Conques and the collegiate of St Sernin at Toulouse. All these buildings, together with the cathedral of Santiago, are architecturally related, having wide aisles around the whole church, including the choir, thus allowing the faithful to proceed past the shrine with its relics, exhibited in the choir behind the main altar. These pilgrimage churches differ in details of structure or decoration, but they clearly follow a plan based on the same principle. The connection between these churches becomes even more evident when, as at Conques, Toulouse and Santiago, they are closely related in sculptural decoration. But although most of these churches are monastic, there is nothing that would prevent this type of church being used for a non-monastic purpose, as at Toulouse and Santiago. It was not monastic association, but the possession of important relics that dictated the choice.

45

43, 44

Cluny: the consummation

However impressive the pilgrimage churches are, it was the third successive building of the abbey church of Cluny, the so-called Cluny III, begun in 1088 by Abbot Hugh, that was one of the greatest churches of medieval times. Financed chiefly by Alfonso VI of Spain, and later by Henry I of England, it represented, as Professor Conant has said, 'the monastic achievement in building better than any other edifice'. Unfortunately, the church and monastic buildings have largely disappeared, but thanks to Conant's excavations and to old descriptions and drawings they are well known. By 1095 the east end, with five altars, was ready for dedication; by 1100 the transepts were ready; by 1115 the west front; and by 1121 the nave was vaulted. The great Abbot Hugh did not see his enterprise finished, for he died in 1109. He was canonized eleven years later at Cluny by Pope Callixtus II. As so often happened with these ambitious medieval buildings, the vaulting of the nave collapsed soon after completion, but it was repaired and the building was consecrated in 1130.

47, 49, 50

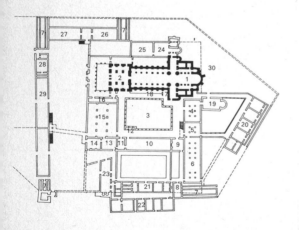

48, 50 Cluny III (*opposite*), was an enlargement of Cluny II (*below*)

Cluny II: 1 church, 2 narthex, 3 cloister, 4 chapter-house, 5, 6 parlour and common room with dorter above, 7 latrines, 8 baths, 9 warming room, 10 refectory, 11 pantry, 12 fountain, 13 kitchen, 14 lay-brothers' kitchen, 15 storehouse, 16 almonry, 17 book-cupboard, 18 scriptorium, 19 Lady Chapel, 20 infirmary, 21 novitiate, 22 workshops, 23 bakery, 24 sacristy, 25 tailors and cobblers, 26, 27 guests, 28 hostel for poor, 29 stables and lay-brothers' quarters, 30 cemetery.

New buildings of Cluny III: 31 church, 32 narthex, 33 Lady Chapel, 34 infirmary court, 35 infirmary, 36 refectory, 37 kitchen, 38 abbot's palace, 39 hospice and stables, 40 cemetery chapel, 41 dorter extension (?), 42 abbot's chapel

47, 49 At the
consecution of
Cluny III in 1095
(*left*), Pope Urban II
stands left of the
altar with Abbot
Hugh to the right.
The church, seen
right from the east,
had towers over the
west end, crossing,
transepts and choir.
The miniature is a
section, from the
western doors and
towers (at the left),
through the
crossing, to the
turreted east end
with its *échelon* of
apses

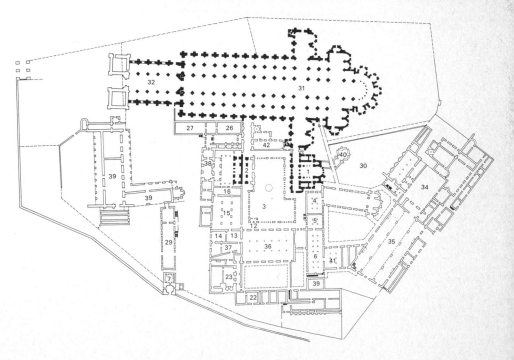

50   The church was a five-aisled basilica with two transepts, an
ambulatory with radiating chapels to the east and a narthex to the
51   west. It was, of course, vaulted throughout and was one of the first
in the West to use pointed arches, which, it is claimed, were introduced from Monte Cassino. The church at Cluny presented the
extraordinary sight of a string of apses, not only clustered around
the curved east end, but also along the east walls of the transepts, of
49   which each had a crossing tower; and there were also towers over
the arms of the western transept. Later, a pair of western towers was
added, and the whole mass of harmoniously arranged forms must
have been breathtaking.

    The church was decorated with wall-paintings, dominated by a
Christ in Majesty in the main apse. Some idea of their quality can
perhaps be gained from the superb contemporary paintings which
105 still survive in the chapel at Berzé-la-Ville, a grange which belonged to Cluny and was a favourite place of retreat for Abbot
Hugh. Nearly five hundred capitals decorated the interior of the
abbey, and those of the ambulatory are still preserved. Much
controversy is centred on the date of the ambulatory capitals, for if
they are as early as *c.* 1095, the date of the consecration of the choir,

51 *Opposite:* This drawing of Cluny III, made shortly before its destruction, shows the pointed arches of the nave arcade, the small triforium and clerestory, the tunnel vaults, crossing lantern and apse. Of the apse the capitals have survived (*right*); its fresco of Christ in Majesty was similar to that in Ill. 105

52 *Right:* a capital from the ambulatory of the third church at Cluny represents the third Tone of the Gregorian chant – a reminder of the important part played by music in the Cluniac liturgy

they are extremely sophisticated in their subject-matter and style. The subjects include allegories such as the Seasons, the Tones of the Gregorian chant and the Virtues. The façade was decorated with a 52 carved portal (before 1115), executed in a more mature style than that of the choir capitals; fragments of this portal were excavated recently by Professor Conant.

When Cluny had recovered from a severe epidemic in 1144, and had further expanded under its last great abbot, Peter the Venerable, the number of monks there was 460. It is no wonder that the buildings required for such a large community were extensive. Novices had their own cloisters and their own living-quarters 50 around it. The lay brothers' quarters were close to the workshops and stables. The monks' cloister was on the south, adjoining the abbey church. This was the centre of the monks' activities outside the choir, and all their living-quarters and meeting-places were placed around it: the chapter-house, the refectory, the dorter, the library. Separate groups of buildings were devoted to guests and to the sick. The first was near the main gate, the other at the opposite end of the building complex, south-east of the abbey church and ominously next to the cemetery. The general layout was essentially

traditional, as is suggested by the similarity of this plan to the
Carolingian plan preserved at St Gall.

The plan of Cluny III was not imitated in France, though the
Cluniac priory at Paray-le-Monial is, in a number of ways, a
smaller version of the great abbey. La Charité-sur-Loire, Souvigny
and St Etienne at Nevers are also buildings which were closely
related to Cluny III without attempting to imitate its grandiose
plan. However, Cluny III was the model for the mother-house of
the English Cluniacs, the priory of Lewes.

Founded in 1077, Lewes was colonized from Cluny and
obviously the monks brought with them the plan of the great
abbey, for Lewes – known from excavations and scanty remains –
repeats, on a more modest scale, the two-transept arrangement of
Cluny as well as the disposition of the monastic buildings, including
the characteristic infirmary chapel.

All English Cluniac priories were lavish in their decoration, but
on the whole, so far as one can judge from their ruins, they were
built in the Anglo-Norman style, with only an occasional detail
derived from the Burgundian mother-house.

Two royal foundations, Reading, founded by Henry I, a great
benefactor of Cluny, and Faversham, founded by Stephen, were
abbeys colonized from Cluny and following the Cluniac customs,
but which never joined the Order.

Cluniac influences in England can be seen not only in Cluniac
priories and in abbeys founded with Cluniac help, but also in
Benedictine churches which had no obvious link with Cluny. This
is particularly true of Christchurch, Canterbury, the metropolitan
church of England, rebuilt at the time when the famous Anselm
was archbishop of this cathedral-abbey. The plan of the new choir,
dedicated in 1130, follows the double-transept arrangement of
Cluny. Some parts of Anselm's church survive today, but the
buildings as a whole can be seen in a famous mid-twelfth-century
drawing now in the library of Trinity College, Cambridge. This
plan had a far-reaching effect on later English architecture of the
Gothic period, when most cathedral churches were built with two
transepts.

Except in England, the effect of Cluny III was not great. By the
time the building was completed, the great age of Cluny was over.
The artistic initiative passed from Burgundy to the French royal

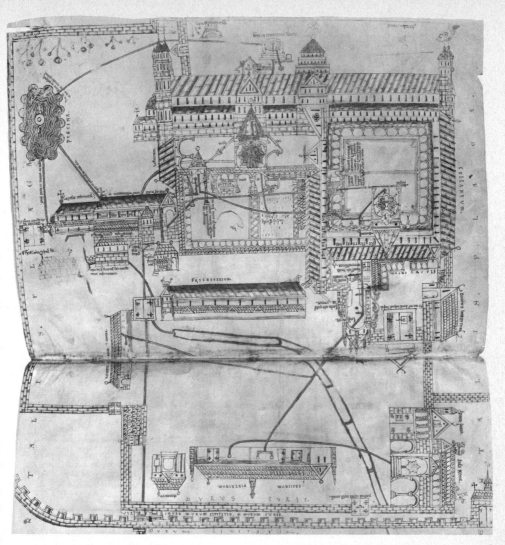

53, 54 An early plan of
Christchurch, Canterbury (*above*),
shows the waterworks supplying
the monastic buildings by the
church, with its two transepts, at
the top. The design, like that of
the Cluniac priory of Lewes (*right*),
though in reverse, follows
Cluny (see Ill. 50)

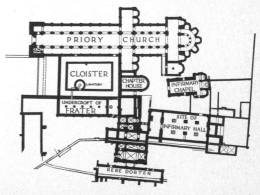

PRIORY CHURCH

CLOISTER
LAVATORY

CHAPTER
HOUSE

INFIRMARY
CHAPEL

UNDERCROFT OF
FRATER

SITE OF
INFIRMARY HALL

RERE DORTER

domain, to Paris and the Ile-de-France. It is to the Benedictine abbey of St Denis and, above all, to its Abbot Suger, that we owe the first Gothic edifice.

Suger (d. 1151) was one of the most outstanding statesmen of the age and well deserved the title of 'Father of his Country' given to him by Louis VII. He was, however, also an abbot devoted to his monks and abbey. St Denis was the burial-place of the French kings, and the abbey had a privileged position amongst all French monasteries. Suger's *Libellus de Consecratione Ecclesiae S. Dionysii* is a priceless document describing the rebuilding of the church, which involved the façade (dedicated in 1140) and the choir (dedicated in 1144). Both works are of the greatest importance to the subsequent history of architecture and sculpture. The façade included 'royal portals' with column-figures which were to change the appearance of churches for many centuries to come. The

55 choir of St Denis is Gothic, and was even more revolutionary in its influence than the façade. No single man effected greater artistic changes in the twelfth century than Abbot Suger. Although he was anxious to be remembered by his gifts to the abbey treasury of

127 objects made from precious stones and metals, his architectural and sculptural innovations are of far greater importance.

The rebuilding of St Denis marks the end of an era. The initiative was passing from monasteries to cities. The monastic school was being gradually replaced by a new scholastic institution, the university. The abbey, once the chief patron of the arts, lost its leadership. Now the city cathedral became the place for experiment and innovation. Itinerant artists had, by now, settled in the towns, and had started to organize themselves into professional guilds. Life was more settled, better organized and more prosperous, and art became technically more accomplished but also more stereotyped. With the decline in the importance of monasteries came the end of Romanesque art.

55 Finished in 1144, the ambulatory built by Abbot Suger at St Denis has slender shafts and pointed rib vaults that are already fully Gothic. Radiating chapels open off to the left

Chapter Three

The Return to Simplicity

Cistercium is the Latin name of Cîteaux, a place in wild and remote country south of Dijon in Burgundy, where the mother-house of a new order was founded in 1098. A group of monks, hoping for a more secluded and stricter life than in their Benedictine abbey at Molesme, settled there under Robert, the abbot of Molesme. He returned to his former abbey, but the community at Cîteaux stayed on, first under Abbot Alberic (d. 1109) and then under Stephen Harding (d. 1134), an English monk from Sherborne.

The idea of founding a new order based on the original Rule of St Benedict, but freed from all its subsequent modifications, was crystallized under Abbot Stephen, who became the new order's able legislator. The *Carta Caritatis*, composed in 1115–18, confirmed by Pope Callixtus II in 1119, and later revised, is the first constitution of the Cistercians – the White Monks as they were to be called, because of their robes. White is the colour of the Virgin Mary, for whom the Cistercians had a particular veneration and to whom all their churches were to be dedicated by the decision of the chapter in 1134. The *Charter of Love* in its final form deals not only with the internal structure of each abbey but also with the relationships that were to exist between all the houses belonging to the Order.

56

In contrast to the autocratic Cluniac organization, in which the abbot of Cluny was the absolute head of all Cluniac priories and was subject only to Rome, the Cistercians were aiming, at least in theory, at something more democratic. The abbot of Cîteaux was to be head of the Order and he was to visit and supervise the daughter-houses; the abbots of these could, in turn, inspect Cîteaux. The abbey from which a new foundation was made had the right to supervise its daughter-house. Each abbey was to be represented at the annual meeting of the General Chapter at Cîteaux, and this chapter was to be the supreme authority of the Order.

56 In this Cistercian miniature the abbots of St Vaast (left) and Cîteaux present their churches to the Virgin, while the scribe Osbert presents the manuscript to the abbot of Cîteaux

The ascetic aims of the founders demanded that the monks should live as far away as possible from the centres of wealth and power. The abbeys were to be built far from cities and settlements, and the monks and lay brothers were themselves to cultivate the land. This meant a return to the earlier Benedictine ideal, which had been abandoned by the Cluniacs. The White Monks, however, went even further, and by shortening and simplifying the liturgy, obtained more time for work in the fields and workshops. It is not surprising that, with their excellent organization and their dedication, they soon became pioneers of agricultural progress throughout Europe.

The four earliest foundations from Cîteaux, the four elder daughters, as they were called, were all in Burgundy: La Ferté founded in 1113, Pontigny in 1114, Clairvaux and Morimond both in 1115. Five years later a dozen Cistercian abbeys were already in existence. In 1128 the first English house, at Waverley in Surrey, was founded; it was the thirty-sixth Cistercian abbey. Further expansion was even more spectacular and by the end of the twelfth century, that is a hundred years after its foundation, the Order had 530 houses; the number rose in the next century to 742. To this impressive total must be added some 900 nunneries, some admittedly very small and not all under the strict Cistercian discipline.

Gradually poverty and simplicity were abandoned, for agricultural exploitation was very profitable with the cheap labour of the lay brothers. Moreover, the expansion of the Order to such distant countries as the Holy Land, Hungary, Portugal and Norway resulted in their exemption from the visitations and attendances of the General Chapter. As a result, discipline was greatly relaxed.

The Cistercian Pope Benedict XII attempted, in 1335, the reform of the Order, but with little success. As riches accumulated, lay rulers resorted to the practice of appointing abbots *in commendam*, that is, the granting of revenues to bishops or even laymen who did not live in the abbey or fulfil the duties of true abbots. A decline set in and the Reformation finally extinguished the Order in many countries. In France, where they were most numerous, the Cistercians had two reforms, leading to the establishment of the Feuillants and the Trappists, but the original Order exists to our day, and, in a number of cases, the White Monks have returned to the sites of former abbeys to refound communities there.

57 St Bernard of Clairvaux, watched by fellow Cistercians, is shown having a vision in this retable of *c.* 1290 from Palma de Mallorca

What the Reformation did to the Cistercian abbeys in England, the Revolution did in France. Most Cistercian abbeys in these two countries are ruins, but in Germany, Italy, Spain and many other countries, Cistercian buildings can still be studied, often in their original medieval form.

The severities of St Bernard

The great age of the White Monks was unquestionably the twelfth century. The need for an order where prayer and work could be practised in equal measure, for the benefit of both soul and body, must have been very genuine. However, the prodigious expansion and influence the Cistercian Order attained in so short a time were due to the leadership of one man, St Bernard. He joined Cîteaux 57 with a group of kinsmen and followers in 1112 and three years later, at the command of Stephen Harding, selected a site for a new abbey, of which he became the first abbot. This was Clairvaux, the abbey which, at the time of Bernard's death in 1153, had no less than sixty-eight dependent abbeys. St Bernard, supported by the popes and especially by the Cistercian Eugenius III, had great power and influence on the religious life of his time. He was a man of action, incessantly travelling across Europe, fighting heresies and preaching the Second Crusade. He was also a reformer, critic and founder of religious orders, a champion of the papacy, a profound thinker and a writer: he left 350 sermons, well over 500 letters and a number of tracts. He was doing all this while at the same time he ruled his abbey of 700 monks.

The Cistercian Order was born out of dissatisfaction with the state of other religious orders, especially the Benedictines and the Cluniacs. It was therefore inevitable that there should be rivalry and tension between them, especially since both the Cluniacs and the Cistercians had their principal houses in Burgundy. St Bernard was neither a tolerant nor a tactful man, and he soon came out into the open with an attack on the Black Monks.

The celebrated *Apologia*, written by St Bernard in 1127, is an indictment of Cluny for its alleged betrayal of the Benedictine ideal. No doubt much of the criticism was justified, especially when applied to Cluny under the misrule of Abbot Pons. Yet, for all their faults, the less austere Cluniacs are more sympathetic than the Cistercians because of their greater humanity and warmth. It was in a Cluniac and not a Cistercian house that Abelard found refuge, and it was Peter the Venerable and not Bernard who comforted him and gave him absolution.

The statutes of the White Monks prohibited painting and sculpture, the employment of colours, precious metals and fine fabrics in their churches. Crucifixes were to be of wood only, chalices of silver and not gold, and elaborate liturgical vestments were to be avoided. Bell-towers of stone were later forbidden. The aim of all this was a return to the simplicity of monastic life such as was intended by St Benedict. But St Bernard was not satisfied with such a limited objective. Since monastic simplicity was desirable, all monastic orders should follow the example of the Cistercians. Thus in his *Apologia* he makes a violent attack on the monastic art of the Benedictine churches. He makes it clear that he was not against the use of art in non-monastic churches, since secular

72

58 The cloister of the Cluniac abbey of Moissac, completed in 1100, is decorated with reliefs of the Apostles, and with single and double capitals that are carved with grotesques as well as Biblical scenes

clergy, 'unable to excite the devotion of carnal folk by spiritual things, do so by bodily adornments'. But in monastic churches the situation is different. Here, lavish adornments are designed not to invite a prayer but to excite vanity and provoke generous offerings. *O vanitas vanitatum, sed non vanior quam insanior* – he exclaims ('O vanity of vanities, yet no more vain than insane'). St Bernard was ready to overlook the relics cased in gold, saints 'gaudily painted', crowns of light 'like cartwheels' studded with precious stones, candelabra like 'trees of massive bronze', and other church adornments, for the sake of the simple and devout congregation.

40

124, 125

However, in the seclusion of the cloister, which is the monks' exclusive domain, the situation is different. Here the Benedictine and Cluniac monk is supposed to pray and study. Yet in St Bernard's day the cloister was the most lavishly decorated structure of the whole monastic complex of buildings. It is enough to recall the Benedictine cloisters of Silos in Spain and of St Aubin at Angers, or the Cluniac marvels such as the cloister at Moissac. Each capital of the arcades is superbly carved and, as if this were not enough, some capitals are doubled, thus multiplying the available surface for carving. And here the tormented imagination and fantasy of the Romanesque sculptor seemed to run wild, unrestrained by any consideration for the sanctity of the site. No wonder that a puritan such as St Bernard could no longer tolerate this: 'What profit is there in those ridiculous monsters, in that marvellous and deformed comeliness, that comely deformity?' In the conclusion of his *Apologia*, St Bernard points out the dangers to which the monks are exposed, for 'we are more tempted to read in the marble than in our books'.

59

58

St Bernard was expressing not only his own opinions, but also the official attitude of his Order. The Cistercian church buildings were, from the start, simple in plan and elevation, and plain in detail. The only dull Romanesque capitals are those in Cistercian buildings. Very early in the history of the Order, a standard church-plan was devised with the result that Cistercian abbeys in England, Portugal or Poland look remarkably similar; similar, that is, in the general form of their design, which was supplied from Burgundy. This 'Bernardine plan' is characterized by its square-ended choir, and a pair or more of barrel-vaulted rectangular chapels on each arm of the transept.

59 The 'comely deformity' that repelled St Bernard: harpies, on a late eleventh-century capital in the cloister of S. Domingo at Silos

60 *Below right:* a mason's mark in the stonework at Senanque

The first Cistercian churches were built largely by the monks themselves, since the sites of their abbeys were so isolated that they could find little local help and, moreover, they often lacked money for the employment of professional masons. But in time, they were to rely chiefly on lay labour. The marks of secular masons found in some of their churches as, for instance, in the late twelfth-century abbey of Senanque (Vaucluse), prove this eloquently. However, it is known from documents that there were architects among Cistercian monks and that their talents were not only used in the abbey to which they belonged: they also were sent to other Cistercian houses to help in building them. At Clairvaux, during the abbacy of St Bernard, there were two monks who were architects – Achard, who presumably supervised the building of the abbey, and Geoffrey of Ainai, sent by St Bernard to Fountains

Abbey in Yorkshire and to Clairmarais in Flanders. Such Cistercian architects helped to transmit Burgundian architectural features to far-off places. On the other hand, by using local builders, Cistercian standard church-plans, elevations and architectural details were frequently modified to conform with the local style of building. For instance, at Fountains Abbey in Yorkshire the nave (after 1135) was not vaulted with the usual barrel but was covered with a flat wooden ceiling, and there was a crossing tower, characteristic of Anglo-Norman churches. As time went on, Burgundian directives were less and less binding and, if local forms were used without excessive ornamentation, there was no discrimination against them.

Since the destruction of Cîteaux and Clairvaux during the French Revolution, Fontenay (c. 1140) is the best-preserved Cistercian abbey in Burgundy. St Bernard must have been well pleased with this abbey, constructed with an almost forbidding

61, 62 The Cistercian ideal appears at Fontenay (*below*, from the north-east), with its towerless church and plain cloister. Fountains (*opposite*, from the south-west) has a similar layout and site, but it had two towers, of which one survives

austerity. The monastic buildings are beautifully grouped around the cloister, which contains only plain capitals so that nothing would distract the monks from prayer and contemplation. The fine workmanship and the rational planning of the whole complex is very striking. The site, like that of almost all Cistercian abbeys, is enchanting, and it incorporates a stream, for it was common practice for the sites of these abbeys to have either a stream or a pond. The natural beauty of Fontenay, Fountains, Fossanova, Bebenhausen and so many other abbeys is unforgettable.

Although some early Cistercian buildings have a half-Gothic appearance, the Cistercians were not architectural innovators. Roche Abbey in Yorkshire may be the first Gothic building in England (*c.* 1160), but it is not entirely original, for it is derived from north-east French non-Cistercian churches.

Rib-vaulting was adopted by the Cistercians about 1150, and was common to all Cistercian buildings throughout Europe erected after this date. But the rib was only one step in the direction of Gothic architecture, and the character of Cistercian churches often remained largely Romanesque, in some instances until the early years of the thirteenth century.

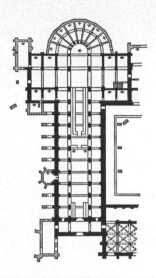

63, 65 Early Cistercian churches had simple, flat east ends – still seen at Fontenay (Ill. 61). At Clairvaux (*left*), and Pontigny (*opposite*), these were soon replaced by curved chevets, still very plain but providing a multitude of chapels

64 *Below:* Chiaravalle in Italy has the traditional flat east end, but differs in being built of brick and in having an ostentatious crossing tower

No sooner had St Bernard died (1153) than the monks set about the task of enlarging the east end of his abbey of Clairvaux. Ready by 1174, the new chevet, with an ambulatory and nine radiating chapels in the most up-to-date north French Gothic style, replaced *63* the modest Bernardine structure. Other Burgundian abbeys soon followed suit. The chevet of Pontigny (*c.* 1186) still survives: it is a *65* beautifully simple and yet elegant structure, in which the Gothic style was admirably adapted to the demands, or rather restrictions, of the Cistercian Rule.

The Cistercians are sometimes credited with the introduction of brick architecture from Italy into Germany, and thence to other parts of eastern and northern Europe. It is true that some of the Cistercian buildings in Lombardy, for example Chiaravalle di Milano, founded by St Bernard in 1135, were built of brick, the *64* material that was natural to the place. It is equally true that many Cistercian abbeys north of the Alps were built of brick, for instance, Chorin in Germany, Sorø in Denmark and Pelplin in the territory of the Teutonic Knights. They were, however, not the only brick buildings there and they were also not the earliest. The question whether in fact the Cistercians were influential in spreading the use of brick outside Italy must remain open.

·I· LEXANDRE
REGINE MORTE IN
superioribz uolumine
demonstrata: se
quentia referi
mus. nichil
aliud festi
nantes in
minime
qequia
de gre
stis
reb;
memorie principendo pretenue. Nam q

66, 67, 68 The close ties between England and Cîteaux in the early twelfth century appear in these three initials, with their similar dragons, foliage and interlace. *Left:* A, from a Canterbury *Josephus* made between 1110 and 1140. *Right:* C, from a Cîteaux manuscript of the *City of God*, 1100–20. *Far right:* R, from St Gregory's *Moralia in Job*, finished at Cîteaux in 1111

Cistercian prosperity – the ideal fades

Unlike the austere Cistercian churches, the early manuscripts produced at Cîteaux are lavishly illuminated. This must have been due to the personal taste of Abbot Stephen Harding, educated at Sherborne Abbey in Dorset, who became abbot of Cîteaux in 1109 and ruled it until 1134. It is generally agreed that the illuminations decorating the books produced at Cîteaux during the early years of Stephen Harding's abbacy are indebted to English illuminations, especially to Canterbury School initials. Stephen left England before the Canterbury painters developed their characteristic designs of 'inhabited' initials, that is initials composed of foliage in which men, animals, birds, grotesque and monstrous creatures climb, fight or devour each other; some of them include humorous or satiric subjects from fables. But it is assumed that he obtained from England books containing some such initials, and that he had them imitated at Cîteaux. These Cistercian illuminations were, however, no mere copies: in fact they are unique examples in the twelfth century of an art that is based on a direct observation of nature. The Cîteaux initials include, besides those which are

66

67–69

inspired by English models, others of quite a different type, for which no models exist anywhere. They depict Cistercian monks observed at their daily occupations around the monastery, felling trees, splitting logs and harvesting. All these initials, painted in light, gay colours, are slightly satirical but, nevertheless, good-humoured and free from malice. It is not surprising that this kind of painting, based on the observation of labour in the woods and fields, should have originated in a monastic order which revived St Benedict's original obligation to work in the fields. To Stephen Harding, brought up in a Benedictine monastery, this was a novel experience: to him and to many other Cistercians with an intel-lectual turn of mind, physical work must at times have presented a comic sight, no doubt provoking a great deal of leg-pulling and jocular comment. At least, the Cîteaux initials express something of this spirit.

70–72

   These extraordinary paintings date from the second decade of the twelfth century, and are undoubtedly connected with the per-sonality of Stephen Harding.

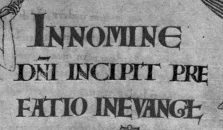

IN NOMINE
DÑI INCIPIT PRE
FATIO INEVANGL
SCDM IOHM.

HIC est iohis euange
lista un' ex discplis
dñi. qui uirgo elect'
a dõ est. que de nup
tijs uolente nubere
uocauit dõ. Cui uirgi
nitatis in hoc duplex testimoniu datur isti e
euanglio. qd' cet'eris dilect' a dño dr'. &
huic matre sua de cruce commendauit dñs.
ut uirgine uirgo seruaret. Deniq; manifestan
in euanglio qd erat ipse incorruptibilis uerbi
op' inchoar. s. solus uerbu carnie factu esse. nec
lum a tenebris compheensu fuisse testatur.
P'miu signu ponens qd inuptijs fecit dñs. ut
ostendens qd ipse legentib; demonstrare. qd'ubi
dñs mutat'. deficere uinu nuptiaru debeat.
& ueterib; inmutatis. noua omia que a xpo
instituunt appareant. Hoc aut euanglii scrip
sit in asia. postea qua in pathmos insula apo
calipsin scripserat. ut cui in pncipio canonis
incorruptibile pncipiu in genesi. & in incorrup
tibilis finis in apocalipsi redderetur.
dicente xpo. Ego sũ a & w. Et hic est iohis qui
sciens supuenisse die recessus sui. conuocatis
discplis suis in epheso. p multa signou experi
menta. pmens xpm. descendens in de fossim se
pulture sue locu. facta oratione posit' est
ad patres suos. ta extraneus a dolore mortis.
qua a corruptione carnis inuenitur alienus.
tam post omis scripsit euanglii. & hoc uirgini
debeatur. Quoy tam ut scriptoy tempoy
dispositio. ut libroy ordinatio. ideo p singla
anob n exponitur. ut sciendi desiderio collo

---

cat o. & querentib; fruc
tus. & dõ magisterii do
trina seruetur. amen.

XPE ÑFAT

INCIP EVA

SCDM IOH

INP CIO

ERAT VE

bu. & uerbu erat apu
& ds erat uerbu. hoc
in pncipio apud dm.
p ipsum facta sunt o
ipso factu est nichil.
tu e. in ipso uita erat.
erat lux hominu. &
tenebris lucet. & tene
n cophender. Fuit hom
a dõ. cui nomen erat ioh
uenit in testimoniu ut
monin phibere de lum
ut oms crederent p ill
erat ille lux. sed
testimoniu phibe
de lumine. Erat
ra. que illumina
homine uenient
mundu. In mundo erat. & mundus p
factus est. & mundus eu n cognouit. Ih
uenit. & sui eu n receperunt. Quotq
receperunt eu. dedit eis potestate fili
fieri his qui credunt in nomine ei. Qui
sanguinib; neq; ex uoluptate carnis nqu
lantate uiri. sed ex dõ nati sunt. Et
caro factu e. & habitauit in nob. & uidim

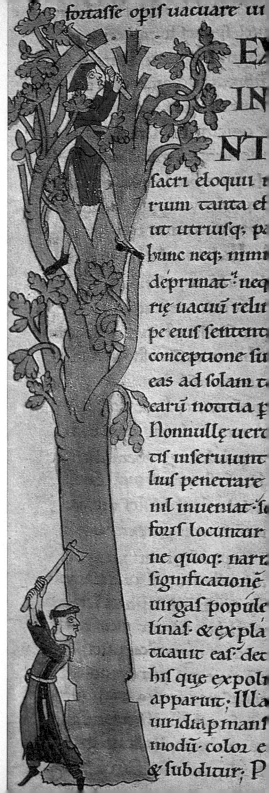

69–72 *Left:* in the Bible of Stephen Harding, of 1109/10, the Evangelist John appears as a white Cistercian (the eagle imprinting its claws on his senses). *Below and right:* Cistercians at work, in rough brown habits – squeezed into initials in a Cîteaux manuscript of the *Moralia in Job* (see Ill. 68)

The illuminations produced at Cîteaux during the second quarter of the century are quite different in character, more austere, dignified and deeply religious. They bear the strong imprint of Byzantine influences. This is very evident in the miniature of the Virgin and Child (Dijon, MS 129, fol. 4v). The moving composition of the mother and child in tender embrace, so intimate and yet hieratic and monumental, is part of a Tree of Jesse, a subject that was the innovation of Romanesque artists (the earliest example is found in a Bohemian manuscript of the late eleventh century). In the feudal system, in which royalty was at the apex of the social structure, it was natural that the idea of Christ's royal descent received much emphasis, and the Tree of Jesse was a form of genealogical table leading from the royal house of Jesse to Christ. That in the Cistercian version of the subject the Virgin Mary received a place of honour is not surprising since the Order was dedicated to her. Rare though this subject was in the twelfth century, it is no accident that it appeared again in a Cîteaux lectionary (Dijon, MS 641, fol. 40v), and there the picture of the Virgin is inscribed *Theotokos*, strongly suggesting that Greek models were available at Cîteaux and affected the style of its painting.

By the middle of the twelfth century the Cistercian Order's uncompromising attitude to figurative art made itself felt even in the field of book decoration, and Cistercian books ceased to receive any but the simplest of ornament. Only for a short time, in the 1170s, was a more ambitious decoration of books once again sponsored by some Cistercian abbeys, notably Pontigny. This time the inspiration was perhaps again English, due to Archbishop Thomas Becket's stay at Pontigny during his exile from England. The illuminations of Pontigny and Canterbury are at this time indistinguishable. The lack of narrative scenes in these illuminations may, however, mean that, in this respect, the inspiration was Cistercian rather than English and that the style was transplanted through the gifts of books sent by Thomas and his secretary, Herbert of Bosham, from France to Canterbury.

The art of illumination was never practised by the Cistercian monks on any large scale, and such luxurious books as were produced at Cîteaux or Pontigny were rather exceptional. When the discipline of the Order was relaxed in the later Middle Ages, illuminations again appeared in Cistercian books, but then commercial

73

56

74

73, 74 Byzantine portrayals of the Virgin in Cîteaux manuscripts.
In the miniature *above right* she is called *Theotokos*; she springs from Jesse
and is surrounded by allusions to her virginity – Moses with the burning
bush, Gideon with the fleece, Daniel, and the fiery furnace

illuminators had, in most cases, to be employed, as in the documented instance of the abbey at Clairmarais in the fifteenth century,
whose abbot had to send to Troyes for an illuminator.

The original simplicity and severity of the Order and its buildings
were difficult to reconcile with the lavish gifts accepted from powerful and rich patrons. Las Huelgas, outside Burgos, a Cistercian
convent founded by Alfonso VIII of Castile as his burial-place, or
Royaumont Abbey, founded in 1228 by St Louis and Alfonso's 75

sister, Blanche of Castile, as the family mausoleum, would have scandalized St Bernard. Royaumont had a cathedral-like plan with an ambulatory and radiating chapels, and a beautifully proportioned elevation typical of the best Parisian buildings in the most up-to-date High Gothic style.

As time went on, not only the buildings but also the furnishings became lavish. In the abbey of Obazine (Corrèze), the tomb of the founder, St Etienne (d. 1159), must have been originally quite simple, but by the third quarter of the thirteenth century it was replaced by a magnificently carved shrine, with an effigy of the saint and scenes from his life. During the first hundred years after the foundation of the Order, the Cistercians were extremely strict in prohibiting any burials in their abbeys except for kings, queens and bishops. The penalties for the rare abuses were very severe, such as the deposition of the abbot and the transfer of the prior and other officials to another abbey. The restrictions became gradually less stringent and when, in 1215, the abbot of Fontfroide was accused by the General Chapter of permitting the burial of a woman in his church, his defence that her name was Reine was accepted and his penalty was only nominal – two days on bread and water and prohibition from using his seat in the stalls for forty days.

75 The elegant refectory at Royaumont, of the second quarter of the thirteenth century, has a particularly well-preserved reader's desk: in his Rule, St Benedict advised that 'there ought always to be reading while the brethren eat at table'

76, 77 Cistercian luxury. *Above:* fourteenth-century stained glass from Amelungsborn. *Right:* the tomb of Jean de Montmirail at Longpont

Royal tombs were allowed, and in churches built especially as mausolea, for example Royaumont, they were of particular magnificence. Not only was St Louis buried there, but also his brother Philippe de France and his children, Louis de France (d. 1260), Blanche and Jean. The founders of Cistercian abbeys were at first not allowed to be buried within the churches, and at Cîteaux the dukes of Burgundy, as founders, had to be buried in a specially built chapel at the entrance. When the restrictions were later disregarded, the abbey became crowded with splendid tombs, including that of Philippe Pot, which was made *c.* 1480, during his lifetime, and is now in the Louvre.

The tombs of the monks were quite plain, but sometimes exceptions were made. For instance, by special permission of the General Chapter in 1253, the monks of Longpont were allowed to erect a tomb in the choir of the abbey into which the body of Jean de Montmirail (d. 1217) was translated. This tomb is known from a watercolour: it represented Jean as a monk and underneath, partly hidden by the arcading, there was another effigy of Jean as a knight, for he had taken the habit of a White Monk late in life. This splendid canopied tomb, richly painted, would certainly have horrified St Bernard.

77

87

78 The
Annunciation, from
a Book of Hours
painted by the
Polish Cistercian
Stanislaus
Samostrzelnik for
Queen Bona Sforza,
wife of Sigismund I

St Bernard would also have disapproved of the lax attitude to other prohibitions. The superb series of fourteenth-century stained glass windows from the Cistercian abbey of Amelungsborn in Saxony illustrates the refined taste of the monks, and suggests that they were prepared to spend large sums of money on decorating their church.

By the end of the Middle Ages, disregard for the earlier prohibitions was complete. The story of the Polish painter Stanislaus Samostrzelnik illustrates the Cistercian mode of life at the end of the fifteenth and beginning of the sixteenth centuries. Born in the mid-1480s, he was, in 1506, a monk at the Cistercian abbey of Mogila near Cracow. At that time he is referred to as *religiosus Stanislaus pictor de Mogila*. Not finding enough interesting work in his abbey, he obtained leave of absence in 1511, and became chaplain to a powerful magnate, who was widely known as a patron of the

76

arts. While in his service, the Cistercian illuminated a number of luxurious books, of which examples survive in Books of Hours in the British Museum and the Bodleian Library, Oxford. But the art *78* of book illumination was becoming obsolete, and Brother Stanislaus eventually returned to the monastic life. Before his death in 1541 he provided a series of wall-paintings for his abbey at Mogila, many of which still survive.

It is difficult to imagine a greater contrast than that between the life of this man, who left his abbey for the more exciting life of a chaplain, and the ideals that prompted the monks of Molesme to seek the solitude of Cîteaux.

Monasteries for men and women

Colleges of clergy serving a cathedral and living under a common discipline existed even before the foundation of the Benedictine Order. As a result of the reform movement of the tenth and eleventh centuries, these colleges of Regular Canons (*canonici regulares*) followed a common code known as the Rule of St Augustine, from which they derived their name, the Augustinian or Austin Canons. Because of their robes they were also called the Black Canons. The Rule was based on the monasticism which St Augustine introduced to North Africa.

Recommended by Rome in 1059, the Augustinian Canons became especially popular in the twelfth century, for quasi-monastic community life, without the rigours of strict monastic discipline, assured for the clergy a more dignified existence than hitherto, and won them general respect and support.

Their earliest establishment in England was at Colchester (*c.* 1095), but the real popularity of the Rule came during the reign of Henry I, when many new foundations were made that were to rise to eminence.

The Black Canons inspired numerous reforms from which new orders were born. The Canons Regular of St Victor in Paris, or Victorines, were founded in 1113 by William of Champeaux, the teacher of Abelard, and numbered among their ranks some of the best scholars and writers of the twelfth century, including Hugh of St Victor, originally from the Augustinian abbey of Hamersleben *79* near Halberstadt, and Richard of St Victor, a Scot. This Order was never very large. An English knight, Oliver de Merlimond, built

for them a church at Shobdon about 1135, but disturbances during the civil war forced them to leave Shobdon for Wigmore, where they founded an abbey. Even here, the scholastic tradition of the Order was observed, and Wigmore could boast a celebrated commentator on the Old Testament, Abbot Andrew (d. 1175).

An order of canons inspired by Cîteaux was founded by St Norbert, a German preacher active in France and a future archbishop of Magdeburg. This was the Premonstratensian Order (White Canons, Norbertines), so called after Prémontré in Champagne where, in 1120, they established their first house. Their Rule was far more austere than that of the Black Canons and included, for instance, the prohibition of meat. In addition to the occupations such as were usual in the Cistercian Order, the White Canons were engaged in parochial duties and missionary work, and that is the reason why they had a particularly large number of houses in Central and Eastern Europe. At the Dissolution there were thirty-one houses (and two nunneries) in England; the Order was introduced into Scotland early by King David.

The only religious order which originated in England was founded in 1131 by St Gilbert, the rector of Sempringham in Lincolnshire. The Order was for both men and women. The nuns were governed by the Rule of St Benedict, the men were Augustinian Canons and acted as chaplains to the nuns. The lay brothers were under the Cistercian discipline. St Gilbert was the first master of this Order, which enjoyed a considerable reputation. Of the twenty-six houses of the Order, eleven were for both men and women. Such double monasteries, in which the monk-priests attended to the needs of nuns, originated in Egypt, and were introduced to Western Europe in the sixth century. There were a number of such monasteries in Gaul, for instance Jouarre. In Spain there existed in the early Middle Ages two hundred double monasteries. St Columbanus was a great supporter of this institution, though there was only one such monastery in Ireland, at Kildare. Introduced into England either from Ireland or Gaul, double monasteries became extremely popular, but they vanished after the Viking invasions.

The successor to these earlier double monasteries was the Order of Fontevrault, confirmed by Pope Paschal II in 1106. This Order owed its origin and rule to Robert of Arbrissel (d. 1117), 'the most

79 Hugh of St Victor, 'the second Augustine', is shown teaching his fellow Victorines in a miniature (painted in the thirteenth century, perhaps at St Albans) from his treatise *De arca morali*

famous and eloquent preacher of those times' as William of Malmesbury calls him. This former anchorite was active in the last years of the eleventh century in Anjou and was followed by crowds of disciples from all classes, including many women. Grants of land and money, in 1100, enabled Robert to set up a permanent monastic community at Fontevrault, south of Angers. This community was to consist of four houses, ruled by an abbess. The first was for contemplative nuns, living under a very strict rule; the second, of St Mary Magdalen, for lay women, mainly reformed sinners; the third for lepers; and the fourth, that of St John the Evangelist, for a small number of priests who were to conduct church services for the other three.

The foundation had a prodigious success and, in less than twenty years, it had a community of three thousand nuns, housed at Fontevrault and its dependencies. By the middle of the twelfth century, there were fifty dependent houses in France alone. One of the English daughter-houses was at Amesbury which, like Fontevrault, became an aristocratic community of nuns who came from the high nobility and abbesses who were frequently of royal blood. Fontevrault became immensely rich through generous gifts from members of the house of Anjou, and the French and English royal families.

80 Ruins of the Premonstratensian abbey of Dryburgh in Scotland, founded about 1150

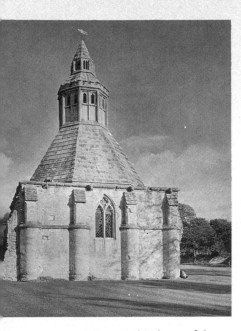

81, 82 Monastic kitchens of the twelfth and fourteenth centuries: the giant at Fontevrault (*right*), and Glastonbury, with a single central chimney

The abbey of Fontevrault is a distinguished Romanesque building, its nave covered with four domes (reconstructed in this century) related to the domed churches in Aquitaine. This impressive structure was imitated by the monks of Leominster Priory in England, which shows traces of an intention to cover the nave with domes – the only instance of this method in England. Fontevrault is known for two other reasons as well. The monastic kitchen there, though *82* much restored, is the most spectacular structure of its kind surviving from the Romanesque period; it is very much larger and more elaborate than the other medieval kitchen, that at Glastonbury Abbey (fourteenth century). The other outstanding feature of *81* Fontevrault is a series of Plantagenet tombs preserved there. Henry II was buried in the abbey church in 1189, Richard the Lion Heart

93

in 1199, Eleanor of Aquitaine, the rejected wife of Henry and mother of Richard, in 1204 and Isabella of Angoulême, widow of King John, in 1246. The effigies of the two kings date from the first years of the thirteenth century and were, no doubt, paid for by Eleanor. Her own tomb is related in style to the sculpture of Chartres of c. 1220 and must have been executed shortly afterwards. The fourth effigy is the only one in the series made of wood and is traditionally identified, but without proof, as that of Isabella of Angoulême. However, the effigy must be contemporary with that of Eleanor and cannot be of Isabella, who did not join the convent until 1243.

Double monasteries were tolerated by the Church but never encouraged, for fear of scandal. That is why the system never became universal.

In the later Middle Ages, about 1346, there was a last attempt to revive double communities, under the rule of St Bridget of Sweden. This Order had a famous house in England, that of Syon, founded by Henry V in 1415 (see below, p. 122).

83, 84 In the ideal convent (*right*, a French miniature of *c.* 1300) nuns attend Mass, above, and follow the priest in procession. *Below:* Poor Clares (Franciscan nuns), *c.* 1430, follow the service in red-bound missals

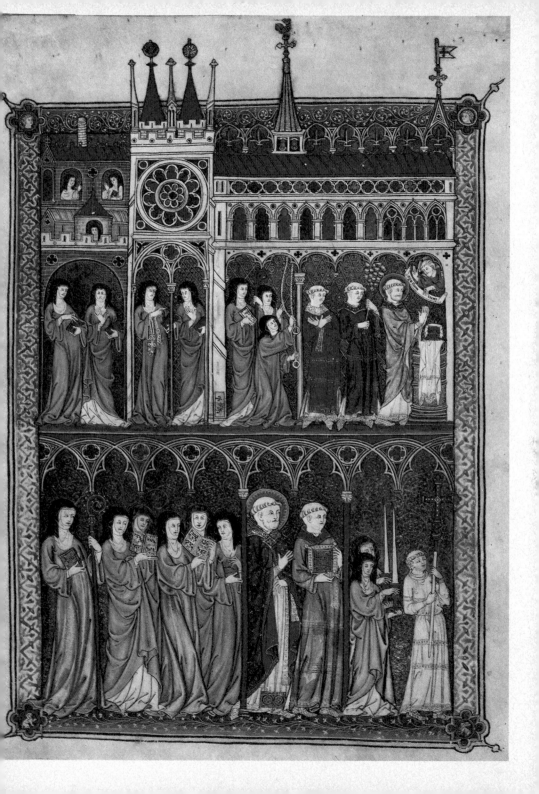

85 St John Gualbert reading to his followers at Vallombrosa: an Italian drawing of *c.* 1400

Chapter Four

Contemplation and Action

The eremitical or contemplative life, frequently practised in Italy in the fifth and sixth centuries, was inspired by the example of Eastern Christendom. It is not surprising that the revival of the eremitical movement, which spread throughout Western Europe in various forms, started in Italy and more especially in the Byzantine south. St Nilus (d. 1005), a Calabrian, who was at first active among Basilian monasteries, later moved north and, in 1004, founded the Basilian monastery at Grottaferrata near Rome. In spite of Latin influences, this monastery remained the centre of Greek life and learning in Italy, and it had as one of its abbots the famous Greek scholar, John Bessarion (d. 1472). Soon after its foundation, Grottaferrata became the centre from which Greek monastic and eremitical traditions spread north.

The Western eremitical movement started, if not as a reaction to Cluny, at least in contrast to its way of life. It was not an accident that St Romuald, the man who founded an order based on the example of the Egyptian hermits, was for a time a Cluniac and abbot of S. Apollinare in Classe, outside his native city of Ravenna. Dissatisfied with the Cluniac life, he resigned the abbacy and withdrew into the marshes of the region to practise severe asceticism. Eventually, he founded a community of hermits at Fonte Avellana in the Apennines, and later a monastery at Camaldoli near Arezzo (*c.* 1012), which gave birth to the Camaldolese Order. Another order, even more severe, was founded by St John Gualbert in 1039. *85* This was the Vallombrosan Order (from Vallombrosa, near Florence) in which perpetual silence, absolute poverty and enclosure were strictly observed. Manual work was prohibited, and the administration of the monastery was entrusted to lay brothers, the *conversi*, a development which practically all other monastic orders were to imitate sooner or later. A rather severe advocate of the eremitical life was Romuald's disciple, Peter Damian. The

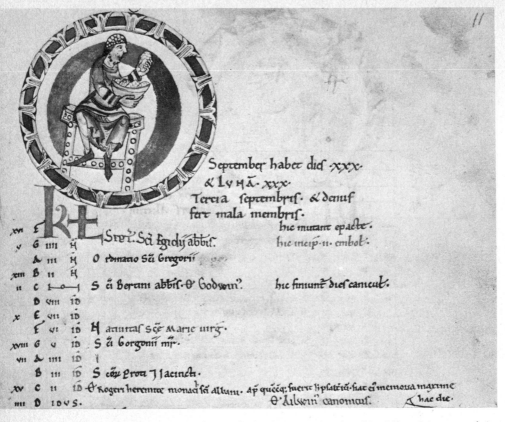

September habet dies xxx.
& Luna xxx.
Tercia septembris. & denus
fert mala membris.

hic mutant epacte.
hic incip. ii. embol.

hic finiunt dies canicul.

86 The death of 'Roger the hermit, monk of St Albans' is entered (at the bottom) in the September calendar of the St Albans Psalter, made for Roger's spiritual disciple Christina

movement soon spread outside Italy and hermits appeared in France, for instance the group led by Robert of La Chaise-Dieu (d. 1067), and in England and Germany.

The Church, on the whole, did not encourage this mode of life, so full of dangers for those who had not had long experience of monastic life. A monk could become a hermit with his abbot's permission, while secular people of both sexes required the bishop's approval. In England alone, several became celebrated for their sanctity, such as St Wulfric of Haselbury (d. 1154) and St Godric of

Finchale (d. 1170), a pirate in his youth, later an indefatigable pilgrim to holy places and a hermit for sixty years. A monk of St Albans Abbey, Roger (d. 1121 or 1122), had the abbot's permission to live in a cell with five companions. For four years, the celebrated recluse Christina lived in an adjoining cell under his spiritual guidance.

In addition to their religious pursuits, the hermits of that period occupied their time with gardening, making garments, combs, pots, mats, baskets and also copying books. Christina was an expert needlewoman, for in 1155 (admittedly when she was already the prioress of Markyate) she sent three mitres and a pair of sandals, beautifully embroidered, to Pope Adrian IV. But it was during her time in the hermitage of Roger that a lavishly illuminated psalter, known as the St Albans Psalter, was made for her. The Egyptian hermits would have been scandalized by such preoccupation with costly objects, since their lives were dedicated to constant deprivation and simplicity.

The desire for a stricter life than that offered by the existing monastic orders continued throughout the Middle Ages, resulting either in reforms of the established orders or in new foundations. Tiron, founded in 1109 by a monk called Bernard and inspired by the early Cistercians, developed into a separate order with numerous dependencies. Its aim was simplicity of liturgy and the performance of manual work, especially through the practice of various crafts.

Another order known for its strictness was that of Grandmont, founded about 1100, where the vows of poverty and silence were observed. To achieve this more completely, the lay brothers were given more initiative in running the administration than in any other order. Grandmont had a comparatively small following and in England, for instance, only three houses were established.

Among the numerous foundations of an eremitical character that came into being in this period was the Norman abbey of Savigny, which began in 1105 as a hermitage, and which eventually adopted a modified Benedictine Rule and the distinctive grey habit. Before long, daughter-houses sprang up in France and the British Isles, but in 1147 these joined the Cistercian Order.

The most successful and lasting of the orders inspired by the Egyptian hermits was that of the Carthusians.

87 The dead Christ, a fragment of
the great Calvary erected by Claus
Sluter in 1395–1403 over the
cloister well of the Charterhouse
of Champmol

88 *Opposite:* the remote site
chosen by St Bruno for the Grande
Chartreuse in 1084 was scarcely
less wild in the early nineteenth
century, when this watercolour
was made. The buildings, often
burnt, were last rebuilt in the late
seventeenth century

The hermits of the Chartreuse

When Philip le Hardi, duke of Burgundy, anticipating the huge
fortune which the inheritance of his wife Margaret was to bring
him, resolved in 1379 to build a mausoleum for the dukes of the
Valois dynasty at Champmol outside his capital, Dijon, he selected
the Carthusian monks to live there as guardians. That a worldly
man like Philip should give preference to this Order is a testimony
to the high reputation for strict observance which the Carthusian
monks enjoyed.

   He built the church and, to the south of it, the chapter-house, the
refectory and other monastic buildings grouped around a small
cloister, while the cells of the twenty-five monks and their prior,
which were in fact small separate houses with little enclosed gardens,
formed a large quadrangle with a cloister walk and a well in the
87   centre, enriched by the famous Calvary of Claus Sluter. Each of the
cells had a painting of the Crucifixion, painted by a team of Flemish
and Dutch artists.

At the time when the Chartreuse was built at Champmol, the Carthusian Order was three hundred years old, but it was still as strict in following the Rule as it had been at the time of its foundation.

The Order was founded by St Bruno of Cologne. He relinquished the post of teacher in the cathedral school at Rheims, and settled in 1084 with some disciples in the wild mountainous region near Grenoble, called the Chartreuse. After a few years, he left France 88 for Italy, never to return, but the community of hermits which he left grew in number, and their customs were codified in the early twelfth century. Many of these were borrowed from the Cistercians – for example, the dress and the external organization centred on the mother-house, the Grande Chartreuse. The life of the monks was solitary, spent in individual cells, which could be left only three times a day for Mass and prayers in the church. Only on feast-days did the monks eat together: even then they maintained silence. The monks who were craftsmen were allowed to practise their art in the cell, and many did. We learn about a Carthusian goldsmith from Ghiberti's *Commentaries*. He was 'a very old Carthusian

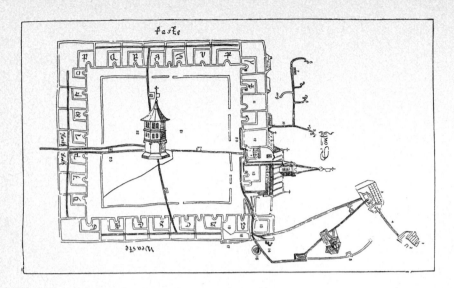

89, 90 The individual houses and gardens that surrounded the cloister of a Charterhouse appear in this plan of the establishment in London, made about 1430 (*above*, redrawn for clarity). The church is at the right, the well-house in the centre. The arrangement is similar in the early Renaissance Certosa di Pavia (*opposite*): the houses, each with a chimney, are reached by separate doors off the cloister

named Fra Jacopo, a goldsmith like his father before him. Fra Jacopo was a draughtsman and took great pleasure in the art of sculpture.' Like Vallombrosan monks, the Carthusians had the help of the lay brothers, the *conversi*, whose buildings ('lower house') were separate from those of the monks ('upper house').

Because of its austerity, the Order never became very popular but, on the other hand, its discipline was always observed; consequently the Carthusians were never in need of reform (*numquam reformata quia numquam difformata*).

The Order was introduced into England by Henry II, it is said in expiation for the murder of Becket. Their first house was at Witham in Somerset where, after initial difficulties, they settled down well under the prior, Hugh, a nobleman from Avalon near Grenoble, who was bishop of Lincoln from 1186 and was canonized in 1220. Little is left of the monastery, save the chapel of the lay brothers. Better preserved is the second (1227) Carthusian foundation in England, at Hinton, where the layout of the quadrangle and the cells is visible and where two medieval buildings survive – the refectory, and the chapter house with library and dovecote above.

Seven Charterhouses, as they were called in England, were built in the fourteenth and fifteenth centuries. Not all were in remote places, and one was built in London in 1349, over the mass grave of the citizens who died during an epidemic of the plague. Of these seven, only the buildings of the Charterhouse of Mount Grace, in Yorkshire, survive.

After a slow start, Charterhouses became, in the fourteenth century, even more popular in Italy than in England, and almost every large town had in its neighbourhood a *Certosa*. The famous Certosa di Pavia was founded in 1396, and owes its repute to its superb buildings and works of art, the majority of which, however, are already in the Renaissance style.

89

90

The warrior monks

The success of the First Crusade, crowned by the capture of Jerusalem in 1099, presented the Christian authorities there with a number of difficult problems. One of these was caused by the pilgrims who, encouraged by the victory, were arriving in large numbers by sea and land. The strenuous and dangerous journey, the climate, and disease were some of the perils which threatened all Westerners who came to the Holy Land. The greatest danger was, however, the journey along the exposed roads of Asia Minor, where the Muslims could strike at will.

It was to deal with this situation, to provide safety, hospitality and medical care for those who came to the Latin kingdom of Jerusalem as pilgrims, that military orders were founded.

The Knights of the Order of the Hospital of St John of Jerusalem, commonly known as Hospitallers, were established about 1110 as a military order following a modified Rule of St Augustine. While in Jerusalem they were attached to the church of St John the Baptist, but after Saladin's victory in 1187 they moved their head-

91 *Left:* in the Great Hospice in their Citadel on Rhodes, originally lined with beds, the Knights of St John cared for the sick and destitute

92 *Right:* Templars, shown riding out to battle, in a late twelfth-century wall-painting from their chapel at Cressac, in western France

quarters to Acre, then to Cyprus (1291–1309), to Rhodes (1310– *91* 1523) and, after 1530, to Malta. Their robes were black with a white cross. The Hospitallers established houses not only in the Holy Land: during the twelfth century, they extended their activities to practically all the countries of Europe.

Their rivals, the Knights Templar – or, for short, Templars – started modestly in 1118 as a confraternity in a house near the Dome of the Rock, the beautiful mosque built on the site of the Temple of *93* Solomon, whence the name of the Order. Ten years later, persuaded by St Bernard, they adopted a rule much influenced by that of the Cistercians. Their robes were white with a red cross on the *92* front. The Templars rose to power with astonishing speed and amassed considerable wealth in all the countries of Europe, settling there to administer their properties. During the thirteenth century they owned nine thousand castles and manors, and it was necessary to divide the Order into nine provinces. Their organization was complex, consisting of different ranks from knights to craftsmen. The expressed purpose of the Order was to defend Jerusalem from the Muslims, but when Jerusalem fell in 1187, the Templars could claim that they were needed to defend those parts of the Holy Land still left in Christian hands. In fact they fought with fanatical courage, and in the final battle at Acre in 1291 the master of the Order was killed. The Templars had many enemies, not only their rivals the Hospitallers, but also those who resented their power and wealth. Their end came when King Philip the Fair, accusing them of immorality and heresy, obtained confessions of guilt by torture. Sixty-eight Templars were burnt in Paris and Senlis, and the possessions of the Order passed to the Hospitallers – that is, what was left of them after the king of France and others had taken their share. Since the Order of the Temple was dissolved by the pope, it ceased to exist in other countries as well.

These two military orders were responsible for a great deal of building throughout Europe. In the Holy Land, their most important buildings were castles, and some of the most spectacular creations of military architecture are due to them. Krak des 97 Chevaliers, Tortosa and Safita are among the most famous. The popular belief is that all the churches built by these orders are based either on the church of the Holy Sepulchre, the Anastasis, a round Constantinian structure (twice burnt and rebuilt), or on the poly- 93, 94 gonal Dome of the Rock, the Muslim mosque used by the Templars as their main church. It is quite true that many of their churches, 95, 96 including the Temples in Paris and London, were circular. This is understandable, and the Hospitallers and Templars were not isolated in their desire to build their churches in imitation of the Holy Sepulchre. In medieval times, however, it was often thought a sufficient imitation simply to include the name 'Holy Sepulchre' in the dedication of a church, without going to the length of imitating the structure of the church in Jerusalem.

All the known English churches of the Templars are circular, but not all their churches and chapels in the Holy Land were of that shape; for example, the chapel at Safita is fitted into a rectangular keep and, in consequence, is also rectangular.

The two principal churches of this Order in the West, in Paris and in London, were both originally circular, but both proved to be too small and had rectangular choirs added later. The Paris rotunda, of mid-twelfth-century date, perished during the French Revolution, but it known from drawings. The London structure was consecrated in 1185 by Heraclius, patriarch of Jerusalem, in the

93, 94 The Dome of the Rock in Jerusalem (*left*), and the Templars' polygonal church at Laon

presence of King Henry II, while the choir was added in 1240. This 'New Temple' replaced, on a new site, a more modest but also round 'Old Temple'. Although much restored, the round nave of the 'New Temple' preserves its original portal, enriched with delicate sculpture, once considered to be a 'Saracenic' work. In truth, it is a typically English doorway in the Transitional style, related to the sculpture of the Augustinian priories at Dunstable and London (St Bartholomew the Great) and of the Benedictine abbey of St Albans. However, the artistic results of the Order's Eastern connections can be seen in another English Templar church, at Garway in Herefordshire. There, between the round nave and the chancel, is an arch enriched with transverse mouldings such as are found in Islamic architecture. 95

The military orders in countries such as Germany, England and France had little justification, save to administer their properties and to recruit members. In Spain and Portugal the situation was different. These countries were in the course of being freed from Muslim rule, and it is, therefore, not surprising that the military orders took a particular interest in them. In fact it has been suggested that the *Codex Callixtinus*, which contains the *Pilgrims' Guide*, was inspired by the Templars. 42

95, 96 The Templars' churches at Garway in England (*left*) and Thomar in Portugal (*right*), both of the twelfth century, include such Moorish ornamental details as transverse mouldings and horseshoe arches. Both churches have round naves

The churches of the military orders on the Peninsula are usually within formidable fortresses. The castle at Thomar in Portugal was begun in 1160 by the Templars under their master, Gualdim Paës, and in 1190 it successfully repulsed a Muslim attack. Within its walls is a circular church of ambitious proportions. The Templars' church of Vera Cruz near Segovia, dedicated in 1208, is circular within and polygonal without. It contained the relics of the True Cross sent from Rome in 1224.

96

The Hospitallers' architecture can best be studied on the island of Rhodes, which the Order occupied during the fourteenth and fifteenth centuries. The city of Rhodes, which contained the various buildings of the Hospitallers, was protected by walls and massive gateways. The Gothic buildings, chiefly southern French in character, included the Great Hospice, for throughout its existence the Order never ceased to take seriously the tasks for which it was founded.

91

The memory of the topography of the various holy sites in Jerusalem was reflected in the arrangement of the buildings in many places. In Cambridge, for instance, the present St John's College occupies the site where the buildings of the Hospitallers originally stood. As if to preserve the familiar topography of the Order's headquarters in Jerusalem, a round church was built (*c.* 1130) nearby, imitating and bearing the name of the church of the Holy Sepulchre.

The Hospitallers, and especially the Templars, because of their connection with the Cistercians, were not great patrons of the arts. Their buildings were utilitarian, and any enrichment (such as the doorway of the Temple in London) very modest. The celebrated tombs in the London Temple are of secular people, not Templars, and thus presumably reflected the taste of the people who paid for them.

97 Krak des Chevaliers, built by the Hospitallers in the twelfth century to guard the vital passes between the East and the Mediterranean coast

109

Amongst the military orders of the Middle Ages, one attained extraordinary power, and was to influence the political scene in Europe to such an extent that the effects are felt to this day. This was the Teutonic Order. It developed into an order out of the Hospital of St Mary of the Germans in Jerusalem, and the temporary hospital which the German merchants established in Acre in 1190. The attendants of this hospital adopted the Rule of the Knights Hospitallers and were recognized by the pope in 1191. Shortly afterwards, with the pope's approval, this charitable Order changed into a military one with the aim of tending the sick and fighting the heathen. Their robes were white with a black cross on the front.

Very soon, about 1200, the Order had possessions in Germany and, shortly afterwards, in Greece, Sicily, Apulia, Moravia and Bohemia. Invited to help defend Hungary in 1211, their members came into conflict with King Andrew II and were promptly expelled. By an act of incalculable folly, the Polish Duke Conrad of Mazovia invited them to his province in 1225 to help to fight the Prussians, who remained heathen in spite of the various attempts to convert them to Christianity.

The Knights arrived in Poland in 1230 and three years later entered Prussia. Within fifty years, by ruthless conquest, they held the whole country and the southern coast of the Baltic from Estonia to Pomerania, settling Germans in newly founded towns such as Memel and Königsberg, or in existing ones such as Gdansk (Danzig), which they annexed. Before long the Order was a powerful and wealthy political state under the nominal suzerainty of Rome and of the German emperor. When Lithuania accepted Christianity in 1386 and became united with Poland, there were no more heathens left to convert and to conquer. The fourteenth century was the period of the Order's greatest prosperity, which ended, however, in the disastrous defeat inflicted in 1410 on the Knights by the Poles and Lithuanians. The Order continued to exist until the Reformation, when it was secularized.

The Teutonic Knights kept the Baltic lands in submission by superior organization based on superb military architecture. All their castles, here as elsewhere, were of brick. The headquarters of 98 the Order were established in Marienburg on the Vistula, and the

98 The fortress of the Teutonic Knights at Marienburg on the Vistula:
the chapel with its high roof can be seen at the right

grand master moved there from Venice in 1309. The fortress of
Marienburg consisted, at that time, of a quadrangle of buildings
for twelve knights, erected about 1280, and a chapel, the whole
complex being defended by strong walls. After 1309 these buildings,
the 'upper castle', were no longer sufficient; they were extensively
rebuilt and enlarged, and a vast 'middle castle' and 'lower castle'
were built. This last was for stores and stables. The 'middle castle'
contained the palatial quarters of the grand master and the high
officials of the Order. The grand master had two refectories – one
for use in the winter and another, for summer, which had two rows
of windows in three of its walls. These buildings, some of the most
luxurious at that time in Europe, in which monastic and military
architecture were blended, suffered severely in the last war. There
can be little doubt that few medieval bodies exploited religion for
their own ends with more cynicism than the Teutonic Knights.

There were many minor military orders, especially in Spain,
besides these three, but they were of local rather than general
interest.

With the end of the twelfth century, the medieval flowering of the monasteries was over. Individual monasteries and even monastic orders continued to maintain high standards, but the spirit which had inspired their founders was lacking. Their wealth did not encourage strict discipline. The custom of obtaining monasteries *in commendam*, in order to use their revenues, brought the final decline. The Fourth Lateran Council of 1215 tried to improve standards by introducing the system of general chapters for all orders on the model of the Cistercians, but this attempt was largely ignored.

The founding of the mendicant orders almost coincided with this Council. The Franciscans were recognized by Innocent III in 1210; the Dominicans came into being between 1206 and 1216, and held their first General Chapter in 1220. The age of the friars was to replace that of the monks.

99   The Franciscan Order or Friars Minor (*fratres minores*), also called the Grey Friars, was, when founded by St Francis, based on the ideal of absolute poverty, not only individual but corporate as well. Begging was preferred to owning money. So strict was the prohibition of any possessions that, at first, even the handling of money was not allowed, except in cases of extreme necessity. This ideal was soon found difficult to observe in an order that increased with great rapidity. There was conflict on this issue even during

99 *Left*: St Francis, canonized in 1228, receiving the stigmata from a seraph: an illustration of *c.* 1300 from a manuscript of the *Golden Legend*, compiled by the Dominican Jacobus de Voragine

100 *Right*: the Franciscan monastery at Assisi is buttressed up on a hilltop, with cells looking out over the valley. The tall church, built in two tiers and dedicated in 1253, is visible at the top right

St Francis's life and, soon after his death, in 1230, a bull of Pope Gregory IX permitted a certain amount of communal property. This was the first of a series of changes that gradually eroded the uncompromising directives of St Francis on this question. But there was always a minority of Friars who felt strongly that this was a betrayal of the founder's high ideals. The conflict between the two points of view continued throughout the Middle Ages, the popes normally taking sides against the stricter party, the 'Spirituals' as they were called. The bitterness of feeling on both sides is well illustrated by the case of William of Ockham, the celebrated Franciscan philosopher, who was excommunicated in 1328 for attacking the pope over the question of poverty.

William was not the only Franciscan scholar of fame. Duns Scotus, and earlier still St Bonaventure, were among the most celebrated in an order which was founded not to cultivate learning, but for preaching and missionary work.

Nothing shows better the difference between the earlier enclosed monasteries and the innovations of the Friars than the Tertiaries, instituted by St Francis for ordinary people living in the world, who wished to practise some of the Franciscan ideals without actually joining the Order. A new spirit of greater humanity and gentleness even in the secular world was the result of the life of St Francis.

The Dominicans, or Black Friars (actually their habits are white, but the cloaks over them black), were founded as an order of *101*

preachers (*Ordo Praedicatorum*) with the aim of converting the Albigensian heretics. Already in St Dominic's lifetime the Order spread far beyond the regions of heresy in southern France. Like the Franciscans, the Black Friars rejected all property, personal and corporate, except the buildings needed to house them. When, however, this prohibition was revoked by Rome in 1465, it was only the official recognition of a state of affairs which had existed for a long time.

102   St Dominic was a canon of Osma, in his native Spain, and that is why he based his rule on that of the Augustinian Canons. The organization of the Order was founded on a series of chapters. The Conventual Chapters sent two representatives to the annual Provincial Chapters, and these, in turn, elected delegates to the supreme body of the Order, the Chapter General. This system of rule by elected bodies, so different from, for instance, the autocratic rule at Cluny, had an influence on the subsequent history of representative institutions, including the English Parliament. On the model of the Franciscans, the Black Friars introduced orders which were under their care, one for contemplative nuns, another for nuns who lived outside a nunnery, and another of Tertiaries.

Founded to combat heresy, the Dominicans remained the guardians of orthodoxy, frequently through the dreaded Inquisition. However, the field in which the Dominicans achieved the most lasting results was that of learning and education. A Dominican who had a great influence on the Christian iconography of the later Middle Ages was Jacobus de Voragine, the author of the *Legenda Aurea* or *Golden Legend*, written between 1255 and 1266, which consists of the lives of the saints. This charming book became
99   widely copied and circulated, and many artists drew from it incidents and details which they translated into visual form in their works.

The two Mendicant Orders were joined by a third in the middle
104   of the thirteenth century. This was the Carmelite Order, which had to retreat, after the collapse of the Crusades, from Mount Carmel in the Holy Land, where it was originally established, to the West. Here it was reorganized as an order of friars, differing from the other two orders in a greater strictness of discipline and self-imposed hardships.

St Francis specifically stated: 'Let the Brothers take great care

114

101, 102 *Right:* St Dominic,
painted within a generation after
his death, probably by Guido da
Siena. *Above:* Dominicans, *c.* 1470

not to receive churches, habitations, and all that men build for them.'
When, in the spring of 1226 during his stay in Tuscany, it became
clear that the saint's death was imminent, he was escorted by armed
knights back to Assisi bypassing big towns, in case he died there
and his body was retained by force for future use as a relic. Francis
died shortly afterwards, having returned to his beloved Portiuncula
outside Assisi. Nobody has ever been canonized with greater speed.
He was declared a saint in 1228 and work was promptly begun on
the magnificent basilica of S. Francesco (dedicated in 1253), and
on another church at Portiuncula. This disregard of the saint's
wishes started the long, but not very distinguished, history of
Franciscan architecture.

The church at Assisi was built on two levels on a simple, aisleless
plan; it is attributed by Vasari to Jacopo da Alemania. Stylistic
connections of this Gothic structure are with Anjou rather than
Germany, and it has been suggested that the architect was not from

100

115

103, 104 *Left:* a cell in S. Marco, painted by the Dominican Fra Angelico. *Above:* detail of the *Reform of the Carmelite Rule,* by Fra Filippo Lippi

Germany proper, but from the French territories within the Empire, such as Provence or Franche-Comté. It is interesting, however, that the earliest stained glass windows in S. Francesco (from before 1253) were by German artists. The simple plan of the mother-church was imitated elsewhere, but neither Franciscans nor Dominicans evolved a single type of church, as did the Cistercians. In France Dominican churches were frequently of the double-nave plan, as at Toulouse. Similar plans were used by friars in Poland and Bohemia, but no single plan predominated there either, and the earliest Franciscan church in Poland, built of brick about 1240 in Cracow, was on a Greek-cross plan. One common characteristic that distinguishes all friaries is their spaciousness, and the slimness of the columns, if any were used, no doubt in order not to obstruct the view of the altar, and to provide the most suitable conditions for preaching.

There was no sculpture and painting which can be called

116

Franciscan, Dominican or Carmelite, though all three orders employed lay painters and sculptors, sometimes the greatest masters of the day, such as Cimabue, who painted at Assisi, and Giotto, who also perhaps painted there (though there is no unanimity on this) and certainly painted in S. Croce in Florence. Occasionally a friar was an artist and was allowed to practise his art without hindrance. The Dominican Fra Angelico not only painted the altarpiece for the church, and devotional pictures on the walls of each cell, in his own monastery of S. Marco in Florence, *103* but was permitted to go to Rome and elsewhere to paint churches. He was allowed to train pupils. The same freedom was given to another famous painter of the same monastery, Fra Bartolommeo. Fra Filippo Lippi entered the Carmelite monastery of S. Maria del Carmine in Florence when he was fifteen years old. He must have learnt his art while in the monastery, perhaps from Masaccio and Masolino. Filippo's fresco in the cloister of his monastery, showing the *Reform of the Carmelite Rule*, is stylistically indebted to these *104* artists. One could cite many more such examples but, in every case, the artist belonged to the local stylistic school and is indistinguishable from secular artists.

A Franciscan artist of extraordinary talent is mentioned by Matthew Paris, who owned a large, exquisite drawing of Christ as the *Son of Man of the Apocalypse* and inscribed it as follows: *Hoc opus fecit Fr. Willelmus de ordine minorum socius beati Francisci secundus in ordine ipso conversacione sanctus nacione Anglicus* ('This work was made by Brother William, a Minor, the companion of St Francis, second to join the Order, holy in life, English by birth.') This English companion of St Francis, known not only from Paris, but also from early Franciscan sources, probably abandoned his art on joining the Order.

Among the rare cases of sculptors who were friars, one stands out particularly. He was the Dominican Fra Guglielmo, the pupil of Nicola Pisano and creator of the pulpit in the church of S. Giovanni Fuorcivitas at Pistoia, and co-sculptor of the celebrated shrine of St Dominic in S. Domenico Maggiore in Bologna.

The contribution of the friars to art and architecture was not comparable with that of the earlier orders. This is understandable. The emphasis in their activities lies elsewhere: in preaching, education and missionary work.

Chapter Five

Monastic Art and Artists

There are no reasons to think that the sculpture in abbeys and priories, any more than their buildings, was the work of monastic craftsmen. This does not mean that there were never any monk-sculptors. Some signatures prove that there were. For instance, 'Guinamundus monachus' executed the tomb of the patron saint of St Front at Périgueux, and 'Martinus monachus' signed the now partly destroyed tomb of St Lazarus at Autun. There are other similar inscriptions and also documentary evidence for the existence of monastic sculptors. However, it can be assumed that, in the majority of cases, these men were trained in their art before taking the vow. The romantic idea that all monastic art was created by monks is totally discredited. But it really matters little whether any given sculpture or other work of art was made by a monk or a layman. The important thing is that the sculpture which decorates a monastic building, a church or a cloister, testifies to the taste of the monks who commissioned the work and paid for it.

Monks were no doubt interested in the iconography of the sculpture decorating their buildings, and it is very probable that they specified what they wanted before the work started. In this sense, they influenced the designs of all the important works of monastic sculpture.

It is inconceivable that the enormous tympanum of Moissac could have been carved without the monks' instructions and probably also sketches. The extraordinary similarity between the quite simple motifs carved on the capitals in the crypt of Canterbury *106* Cathedral and the initials in the books illuminated in the monastic scriptorium at Canterbury strongly suggests that the designs for *66* the capitals came from the same scriptorium. This is rather an exceptional case, and it must not be assumed that the medieval sculptor was merely executing in stone what the monks had designed for him in a pattern-book.

Sculptors must often have been illiterate. At Vignory, which was

119

105 Christ enthroned gazes down from the apse of the Cluniac grange of Berzé-la-Ville, in an early twelfth-century fresco based on that in the great apse at Cluny (Ill. 51)

106, 107 Models for the crypt capitals at Canterbury (*left*), of *c.* 1120, seem to have come from the scriptorium (see Ill. 66). *Above:* a sculptor at Vignory reversed his pattern, and faithfully copied the inscription back to front

107 a priory of St Bénigne at Dijon, a mid-eleventh-century capital carved with a lion is inscribed in reverse, O∃⅃, probably the result of copying a pattern against the light. They naturally needed guidance from the monks in theological matters. The tympanum at Conques, one of the largest carved in the twelfth century, with its crowd of figures and elaborate Latin inscriptions, is even more unthinkable without the learned help of the monks than that at Moissac.

Most wall-paintings were presumably done by lay artists, who had to be mobile, moving from place to place as commissions required. It would have been impossible for a monk to spend his life in this way. Occasionally, monumental paintings were the work of monks. William, the favourite painter of Henry III of England, was a monk of Westminster. But, not surprisingly, he had been a practising painter before becoming a monk.

Much the same situation existed in painting as in sculpture: the monasteries provided ideas, especially the subject-matter, but the monks seldom did the work themselves. The monasteries were also the most important patrons for many centuries. The best Romanesque wall-paintings are always to be found in monastic churches.
105 St Savin-sur-Gartempe, Berzé-la-Ville, S. Clemente in Rome, S. Angelo in Formis, Tahul, León, Winchester, Reichenau and hundreds of other famous cycles of wall-paintings are all in monastic churches.

There is very seldom any mention in documents of a nun who was a painter, such as Clara Gatterstedt from the convent of St

James at Kreuzberg, who, in the fourteenth century, painted portraits of the abbots of Fulda. It will be seen below that occasionally nuns painted manuscripts. It was, however, needlework in all its forms which was the art practised most frequently by the nuns. In the lives of female saints there is often reference to embroidery made in nunneries. The Abbess Cunegunde of Göss in Austria and her nuns embroidered, in the thirteenth century, the antependium for their altar and a whole range of liturgical vestments. Sometimes

108 A detail of the Syon Cope, embroidered *c.* 1300–20 in silk and metal thread: the Disciples carry the Virgin's body to burial

109 Abbess Cunegunde of Göss in Austria is recorded as an embroidress of skill. She also commissioned a Passionary, about 1320, which includes this fine drawing of Christ with the stigmata embracing His Mother

the work was less serious and, in the same century, Archbishop Rigaud of Rouen repeatedly had to forbid the nuns of St Amand to embroider their own purses and veils.

English Gothic embroidery, the *opus anglicanum*, was highly valued all over Europe and many beautiful examples are preserved in Continental churches. The Syon Cope (now in the Victoria and Albert Museum in London), made in the early fourteenth century, is a superb example of this type of embroidery, being worked with numerous Biblical subjects and heraldic devices. This cope is not only of artistic but also of historical interest, for it belonged to, though it was not made for, the Brigittine convent of Syon, the foundation of Henry V in 1415. The nuns went into exile during the reign of Elizabeth I, but when the convent was reborn in 1810, the cope was brought back.

108

Another English embroidery, also worked in the early fourteenth century and now in the same museum, an antependium or altar frontal, is unique, for it is the only signed *opus anglicanum* (though the signature is now much decayed). It was made by the nun Joanna of Beverley. However, it appears that the greater part of the high-quality embroidery done during the Middle Ages was not the work of nuns but of professional workshops under the direction of men, in which both men and women were employed.

It can be said, without much exaggeration, that until the development of the universities the intellectual life of Europe was based on the monasteries. The Benedictine Rule, because of its balance between prayer, work and study, provided very suitable conditions for the pursuit of learning. The Cluniacs were too occupied with *47,* liturgical duties and the Cistercians with manual work to be able to *70–72* devote much time to study, and thus they produced only a comparatively small number of writers and thinkers of distinction. Some orders established traditions of learning. For instance, in the twelfth century, the Victorines were outstanding for the number of distinguished theologians among their members, but the Order *79* that was most particularly devoted to study so as to be able to preach effectively and, above all, to defend orthodoxy against the heretics, was the Dominican. However, their learning is more part *101, 102* of the history of the universities than of the monasteries.

For intellectual pursuits books as well as time were needed: here the old Benedictine houses, in which books had accumulated for centuries, had a great advantage. But books were, of course, being copied continuously in the scriptoria attached to every monastery. There letters were written, documents prepared and books for the choir and cloister copied.

In big monasteries, in the eleventh and twelfth centuries, there would be up to a dozen copyists; but during the twelfth century more and more professional lay scribes were available, and thus monasteries could now buy books. It has been calculated that an average copyist would produce three to six folios a day, and that to copy the Bible one whole year was required. Sometimes monks from other monasteries would come to copy a precious text. In other cases, books were lent for copying. The *Magna Vita* of St Hugh of Lincoln tells of one such loan, though a rather exceptional one. On hearing of a very splendid Bible just produced by the Benedictine monks of Winchester cathedral-monastery, Henry II persuaded them to lend the book to the newly founded Carthusian house at Witham. This book was presumably the celebrated Winchester Bible.

The number of books in some monastic libraries is known from catalogues, or rather book-lists, which the librarians kept. Cluny had, in the twelfth century, about 570 books, Reichenau about 1,000, the monastery of Christchurch Cathedral at Canterbury 600. This last library contained 4,000 books at the time of the Dissolution. It must be remembered, however, that medieval volumes usually contained at least three books bound together.

One of the artistic results of the monastic reform movement of the tenth and eleventh centuries was the emergence of a new type of small illustrated book, the *libellus*, devoted to the life and miracles of local saints, with prayers and a liturgical text. The cult of saints and their relics was, of course, a popular form of devotion from the earliest days of the Church, and there were frequently representations in many media of their lives and miracles. There were also numerous books devoted to biographies of individual or groups of saints. Some such books might have been illustrated, but nothing has survived to prove this. The illustrated *libelli* appeared in the tenth century and were increasingly popular throughout the eleventh and twelfth centuries, only to fall out of use in the thirteenth. Professor Wormald, who was the first to study these books as a group, came to the striking conclusion that their sudden popularity was due to a new pride in local saints, resulting from the reform and restoration of so many monastic houses. 'The illustrated *libellus* was a mirror for monks, part of the relics of the monastery.' It was kept not in the library in the cloister, but in the treasury. All illustrated *libelli* are monastic, from such abbeys as Monte Cassino, Fulda, St Bertin, St Quentin, St Amand, St Aubin at Angers, Werden, Ste Croix at Poitiers, St Maur-des-Fossés, Durham and Bury St Edmunds. They are often sumptuously painted by great artists: the *Life of St Edmund*, for example, has thirty-two full-page miniatures.

Many other books were illustrated by initials or pictures. The scribe and the illuminator were usually different people, and one book was frequently the work of several scribes and illuminators. The Winchester Bible, mentioned above, is a striking example of a splendid work on which several artists were engaged, each employing a style of his own. This exceptionally rich manuscript must have taken several years to complete.

The question of the extent to which the art of illumination was practised by monks is impossible to answer. Of course, in the early Middle Ages, monasteries were the only repository of books, and

112, 113

QUIESCITINMONTE
TUO :
NCRIDITURSINE
CULA ·ETOPERATUR
TITIAM ·
OQUITURUERITA
INCORDISUO ·
INONECITDOLU
INGUASUA ·

SUSPROXIMOSSUOS ·
ADNIHILUMDEDUCTUS
ESTINCONSPECTUEIUS
MALIGNUS · TIMENTES
AUTEMDNMGLORIFICAT
QUIIURATPROXIMO
SUOETNONDECEPIT ·
QUIPECUNIAMSUA
NONDEDITADUSURAM

QUIFACITHAEC · NON
MOUEBITURINAETERNUM :

110, 111 Illustration to Psalm 16, from the Utrecht Psalter of 816/23
(*above*), and the Eadwine Psalter of *c.* 1150. The Canterbury artist has
faithfully reproduced the sometimes odd images of the original: thus
Christ in Limbo and the Maries at the tomb (left and centre) illustrate the
verse, 'thou wilt not leave my soul in hell; neither wilt thou suffer thine
Holy One to see corruption.' But the freedom of drawing and the sense
of space have disappeared

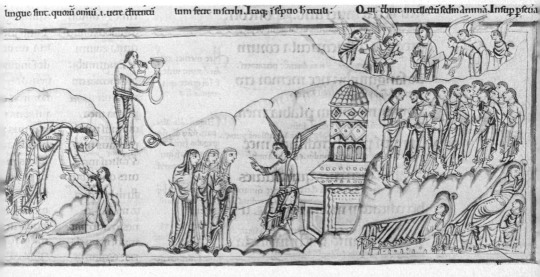

monks the only people who copied them and illuminated them.
We have already mentioned instances of copying books at Canterbury and in Northumbria from originals which were brought from
Italy. And the copying of books, without which no services could
be conducted and no monastic life could exist, went on everywhere,
all the time. Books were easily transportable, and if they were
illuminated the art styles of one centre could easily have been
transplanted by this means to another. There are countless examples
of this migration of styles, often over great distances as, for instance,
in the case of the early twelfth-century Bible of the Grande Chartreuse (Grenoble, MS 17), which is decorated with initials that are
characteristic of Monte Cassino.

14, 15,
19, 20

Occasionally, a single illuminated manuscript was influential for
centuries. A striking example of this is the case of the Utrecht
Psalter (Utrecht, University Library, Script. eccl. 484), the Carolingian masterpiece produced at Rheims between 816 and 823, which
is illustrated by small, illusionistic drawings, influenced by the art
of Late Antiquity. This book was, by the tenth century, in the
possession of Christchurch, Canterbury and was copied there no
less than three times, c. 1000, c. 1150 and c. 1200. The impact of
these Carolingian drawings on the 'Winchester School' style was
very profound; it is almost tempting to say decisive.

110

111
30

It is not known who made the earliest and latest copies of the
Utrecht Psalter at Canterbury, but it is assumed that they were
made by the monks of Christchurch. We know, for certain, that
the scribe of the mid-twelfth-century copy was the monk Eadwine,
whose portrait occupies a whole page of folio 283v, with an
immoderate inscription of self-praise, in complete disregard of the
Rule (Chapter LVII) which states: 'Artificers . . . shall practise their
special arts with all humility.'

The scribe of the Eadwine Psalter (Cambridge, Trinity College,
MS R. 17. 1), was a monk, but there is no proof that the author of
the tinted drawings was also a monk. Perhaps he was a hired layman and that is why his name is not mentioned. It has been suggested that another contemporary Christchurch book, in two
volumes, the Dover Bible (Cambridge, Corpus Christi College,
MSS 3 and 4), was in part written by Eadwine and illuminated by
the same painter who illustrated the Eadwine Psalter. As it happens,
one of the initials in the Dover Bible shows a lay illuminator painting

111

112, 113 Initials from the
Winchester Bible, of *c.* 1160–70,
by the Master of the Leaping
Figures (*right*), and the Master of
the Gothic Majesty

the initial, assisted by an apprentice grinding colours. It may thus *114*
be assumed that this is a self-portrait, and that the two famous
twelfth-century books produced in one of the most important of
English monasteries were the result of collaboration between the
scribe-monk and the lay painter. Whether or not this was a common
practice is not known, but it is significant that in another instance,
and from about the same time but in a place far away from England,
a similar type of collaboration can be deduced. It is in a Bohemian
manuscript now in Stockholm (Royal Library, MS A 144, fol.
34v) where, on the margin below a full-page miniature, is a
representation of a monk writing the text, while a lay painter
'Hildebertus pictor' and his assistant 'Everwinus' are shown with *116*
their paint pots. (A similar scene by the same hand appears in a
manuscript in Prague.)

Representations of monks as painters are not frequent. One such
Norman monk-artist of about the year 1100 not only painted his
self-portrait but also signed his name, Hugo pictor, and *Imago
pictoris et illuminatoris huius operis* (Oxford, Bodleian Library,
MS Bodley 717, fol. 287v). A curious portrait of a monk who was a
painter or a scribe is found in a Durham manuscript (Cathedral
Library, MS B. 11. 13, fol. 102), dating from before 1088: the
kneeling monk 'Robertus Beniamin' is shown with a nimbus as if *115*
he were a saint!

127

For some obscure reason, Spanish manuscripts provide more information about scribes and painters than works in any other country. Moreover, Spanish books are also frequently dated very precisely. It has been calculated that, of just over two hundred surviving books with miniatures produced in Spain during the

114–17 ARTISTS IN THEIR WORK. *Left:* painters, in the twelfth-century Dover Bible. *Above:* 'Robertus Beniamin', with a halo, in an eleventh-century manuscript from Durham. *Below:* 'Everwinus' holds out paint-pots for 'H[ildebertus] pictor', watched by the scribe (1136). *Opposite:* tenth-century copyists in the scriptorium of S. Salvador de Tábara

tenth and eleventh centuries, more than a quarter give information about their scribes and painters. As in the early Middle Ages, they are all written and illuminated by monks. One such book, a copy of the *Commentary on the Apocalypse* by Beatus of Liébana, a monk who lived in the eighth century, not only gives information about the monastery where the book was made (San Salvador de Tábara), but also gives the names of two painters, the priest Magius, who died in 968 before completing the work, and Emeterius, who finished it in three months, from May to July, 970. A human touch is added by a miniature showing a scriptorium adjoining a tower, with a caption: 'Thou lofty tower of Tábara made of stone! *117* There, over thy first roof Emeterius sat for three months bowed down and racked in every limb by the copying.'

It is also in Spain, at about the same time, that the name of a woman, Erde, is mentioned as a painter of another Beatus manuscript. She collaborated in this work with Emeterius, and it has been suggested that these two were members of a double monastery.

118 This copy of the destroyed *Hortus Deliciarum* of Herrad of Landsberg shows the convent's founder handing the key to its patron, St Odile, watched by the nuns

This information is unique, but perhaps the practice of book-painting by nuns was not. On this no further information exists, though, of course, nuns as well as monks needed books for reading, and at times composed books or commissioned them for their specific use. The celebrated *Hortus Deliciarum*, an encyclopedia written for her nuns by Abbess Herrad of Ste Odile in Alsace, between 1167 and 1195, illuminated by a vast number of drawings of the highest quality, is an example of the intellectual and artistic climate of some of the convents.

118

Matthew Paris (d. 1259), a Benedictine monk of St Albans, is probably the most celebrated of English monastic artists and historians. The outline drawings illustrating his *Chronica Majora* and other of his historical writings are perhaps not great works of art, but they have a great liveliness and freedom. His enormous output required assistants who absorbed his style quite well. On the whole, it is safe to assume that, if manuscripts associated with

119, 126

119 A drawing by Matthew Paris representing the shrine of St Alban in Offa's time may show the work of the twelfth-century craftsman Anketyl

an abbey show a stylistic continuity, or at least a relationship with each other, they were painted in the monastic scriptorium of that abbey. For instance, the manuscripts of the eleventh and twelfth centuries from Monte Cassino have such an unmistakable stylistic similarity that it is clear they were decorated in one scriptorium, even if many years separate them. The same is true of manuscripts from many other centres, including Canterbury, Limoges and Regensburg.

The difficulty in deciding whether any particular book was made commercially for the use of a monastery, or in that monastery by its own monks, is very great. As time went on, the chance that the work might have been made in the monastic scriptorium diminishes. Yet even in the early fifteenth century there were serious monastic painters such as Don Simone (d. *c.* 1426) and, above all, Lorenzo Monaco (d. 1425), both natives of Siena and both Camaldolese monks. In the later Middle Ages, it is easier to find a manuscript in which a monk is ridiculed than one in which he displays his skill. In a book painted for the Augustinian Canons of St Bartholomew's, Smithfield, in London, a comic marginal painting shows a monk and a woman in the stocks, for a sin too obvious to require a caption. In another famous manuscript, the Queen Mary Psalter, nuns and monks are shown playing musical instruments and dancing together. This is truly a world far removed from the saintly reformers of an earlier age.

120, 121 Wry views of monastic life *c.* 1300, from Queen Mary's Psalter (*right*), and the Smithfield Decretals

The author of the well-known manual of art entitled *Schedula Diversarum Artium*, who wrote under the name of Theophilus, is frequently identified as Roger, a monk of Helmarshausen. Roger was a monk-goldsmith in a monastery which was, in the twelfth century, an important art centre. Whether Theophilus and Roger of Helmarshausen were one and the same person cannot be proved, but what is important is the fact that Theophilus was a monk as well as being a man who knew very intimately every artistic craft.

122

This evidence, together with many accounts of metalwork which was done by monks, means that this art was practised in *some* monasteries. Metalwork was obviously considered a noble craft, since so many chroniclers attribute the practice of it to important saints, not only to St Eligius (Eloi), bishop of Noyon, who was the patron saint of metalworkers, but also, at a much later date, to St Dunstan and to St Bernward of Hildesheim, whose candlesticks were said to have been found in his coffin when it was opened in the twelfth century. Many of these accounts, however, seem to contain a considerable element of fiction.

123

When in 1198 the shrine of St Edmund was slightly damaged by fire at Bury St Edmunds, and the monks wanted to repair it during the night, before the arrival of the pilgrims next morning 'to avoid the scandal of the matter', they had to send to the town for a goldsmith, which shows that there was nobody in that large and rich monastery who could do this work.

A fair amount of documentary evidence exists, covering the twelfth and thirteenth centuries, concerning goldsmiths at work in the important Benedictine abbey of St Albans. Some of this evidence is of particular value, since it is supplied by the historian of the abbey, Matthew Paris, who was himself, among his other accomplishments, a goldsmith. Matthew Paris was educated in the abbey and became a monk there in 1217. After his death, in 1259, he was described not only as a 'magnificent historian and chronicler', but as having 'such skill in the working of gold or silver and other metal, and in painting pictures, that it is thought that there has been no equal to him since in the Latin world.' From him and from other sources, we learn, for instance, about a goldsmith called Anketyl who, having previously spent some years in the service of the king of Denmark, became a monk of St Albans and, between 1124 and 1129, made, with the help of a lay assistant, the shrine of the patron of the abbey, studded with antique cameos excavated at various times in the near-by site of the Roman town of Verulamium. Other works made at that time, and possibly by Anketyl, include candlesticks, an arm-reliquary, and a gold and silver altarpiece for the high altar.

Each abbot of St Albans made gifts of precious objects to the abbey and, for instance, Abbot Robert de Gorham (1151–67), possibly from Gorron in Maine, gave a silver censer, a vase for the Eucharist and a silver corona of hanging lights. The next abbot, Simon, gave to his church a gilt cross and a vessel with cast reliefs; he commissioned from Master John of St Albans, in about 1170, a splendid silver-gilt cover for the shrine of the patron saint, and from Master Baldwin a large chalice of gold, enriched with precious stones and ornamental flowers. Baldwin further made a ciborium and various other less costly chalices. Under Abbot Warin (1183–95) a shrine of gold and silver for the relics of St Amphibalus and his companions was made, and this was decorated with the scene of the saint's martyrdom.

About the turn of the century, an artist who was a goldsmith, sculptor and painter became a monk of St Albans; this was Walter of Colchester. Eventually (*c.* 1215) he was made a sacrist, and he

122 Detail showing an emperor, from the silver portable altar made about 1100 by Roger of Helmarshausen – perhaps the writer Theophilus – for Abdinghof Abbey, now in Paderborn Cathedral

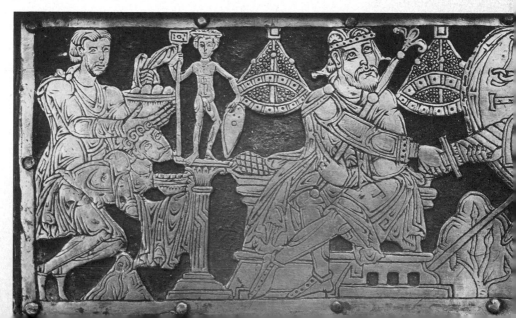

123, 124, 125 *Left:* a pair of bronze candlesticks attributed to Bishop Bernward of Hildesheim, *c.* 1015. *Above:* a reconstruction of the great candlestick of St Remi at Rheims, *c.* 1150, three times the height of a man. *Opposite:* detail of the Trivulzio Candlestick in Milan, *c.* 1200, showing the type of ornament – figures and scrolls – common to all three examples

died in 1248. In his own abbey, he made the antependium for the high altar and two silver-gilt book covers decorated with figures. His fame must have been very great, for he was responsible, in collaboration with Master Elias of Dereham, for making the shrine of St Thomas of Canterbury, which was ready for the translation of the relics and consecration of the Canterbury choir in 1220. Walter of Colchester's nephew, Richard, made for the abbey *magnum candelabrum* – a great candlestick. English documents frequently mention such bronze candlesticks, usually seven-branched, made in imitation of that which Solomon had made for the Temple (known to medieval men from its representation on the Arch of Titus in Rome). Such candlesticks already existed in Carolingian times, and there are records of two, one at Aniane and another at Fulda. The earliest surviving example, from the beginning of the eleventh century, is in the Münster at Essen. In 1035, King Cnut gave such a candlestick to Winchester. Durham

Cathedral had a candlestick with branches stretching across the choir from one wall to another. There was a candlestick called 'Jesse', of foreign workmanship, in St Augustine's, Canterbury. The candlestick at Bury St Edmunds, which perished in the fire of 1465, was inscribed with verses which suggest that it had figures from the Creation and the Fall on it. Seven-branched candlesticks, all of the twelfth century, survive at Brunswick, Klosterneuburg and Prague; one in Milan is possibly of English workmanship; a foot is all that remains of an enormous one from the abbey of St Remi at Rheims.

125

124

The popularity of these candlesticks during the Middle Ages was due not only to the fact that they imitated the furniture of the Temple of Solomon, to which Christian churches were frequently compared, but also to the symbolic interpretation of their seven lights as the seven gifts of the Holy Spirit, mentioned in the Vision of Isaiah (Chapter XI, 1–2), the vision which also became the source of the 'Tree of Jesse'.

74

None of these rich treasures which once belonged to St Albans Abbey has survived but, thanks to Matthew Paris's drawings, some information can be gathered about the shrine of St Alban. One of his drawings (Dublin, Trinity College, MS E. 1 40, fol. 61) depicts the shrine in the days of Offa, but it has been convincingly argued that, in fact, it is a schematic representation of Anketyl's work. Matthew

119

Paris also left coloured drawings of jewels which, in his time, belonged to St Albans (British Museum, MS Cotton Nero D. 1,

fol. 146 recto and verso) – a unique document of its kind.

From the example of St Albans, several interesting general conclusions can be drawn. First of all about monks as artists. Except for Matthew Paris himself, who entered the monastery young and must have learnt his artistic skill while in the cloister, most of the other monks who were artists there acquired their crafts before entering the monastery. But the activity of monk-artists was not sufficient for the amount of work required, and it was obviously a common practice in twelfth-century monasteries to entrust a considerable amount of artistic work to laymen. Another important observation can be made about at least some of the artists of the period: as in the case of Walter of Colchester and of Matthew Paris himself, it was not infrequent for an artist to be skilful in many fields, to be at the same time a painter, sculptor and metalworker. This was certainly not the exclusive peculiarity of artists connected with St Albans Abbey, but was a widespread phenomenon. It is often said that one branch of medieval art influenced another, for instance that illuminated manuscripts influenced sculpture. But if it is borne in mind that many artists were capable of illuminating manuscripts, executing wall-paintings, carving in wood and stone, casting in bronze and making enamels and stained glass, the stylistic relation between different media becomes much more understandable and natural. The manual of Theophilus shows what a great accumulation of practical knowledge in many skills he acquired, and wished to pass on to others.

With the great age of urban cathedrals in the thirteenth century, all this was to change. Enormous expanses of stained glass required specialists who would devote their entire time to this work and, similarly, row upon row of statuary on cathedral façades needed full-time specialists in this form of artistic production. The painting of books passed, gradually, almost entirely into the hands of lay craftsmen working to order. The great age of monastic art was over. The elegance and the prettiness of Parisian books, ivories and metalwork of the thirteenth century illustrate this change eloquently, for Gothic art was certainly not of monastic inspiration.

There can be no doubt that during the Middle Ages metal objects were the most valued of all artistic works, and this was not

126, 127 *Above left:* an Imperial Roman cameo from the treasure of St Albans, drawn by Matthew Paris. *Above right:* detail of Abbot Suger's chalice, a Roman sardonyx set in gold with gems

only on account of the precious metals, stones and gems used. Shrines, which were usually made of gold, were venerated because of their contents. The naïve yet majestic figure of Ste Foy at Conques was found, when recently restored, to have additions made at eight different periods, as if almost every generation of monks had been anxious to contribute something to the precious statue-reliquary.

The altar-frontals of gold, the altar candlesticks and crosses, the gold covers studded with precious stones on liturgical books, the chalices and patens, the reliquaries and later the monstrances – *127* these were all objects of cult or connected with Divine Service and, by virtue of this connection, they were especially precious. The material value was not, however, without its importance and such objects were, in times of need, pawned and even melted down. The wonderful skill involved in fashioning them was obviously greatly admired. Abbot Suger, when describing additions to the golden altar of St Denis, says of the chased relief work that it is as admirable for its form as for its material. In another place, when he writes about gilt-bronze doors, he quotes the inscription which he placed on them and which begins with the words: 'Whoever thou art, if thou seekest to extol the glory of these doors, marvel not at the gold and the expense but at the craftsmanship of the work.' Even St Bernard, that severe critic of the arts, when talking of metal objects, uses such expressions as 'fashioned with marvellous subtlety of art, and glistening brightly with gems', for even he could not hide his admiration for their beauty and artistry.

137

Select Bibliography

AUBERT, M. *L'Architecture cistercienne en France*, 2nd ed., 2 vols. (Paris, 1947)

BENNETT, R. F. *The Early Dominicans* (Cambridge, 1937)

BERTAUX, E. *L'Art dans l'Italie méridionale* (Paris, 1904)

BROOKE, C. *The Twelfth Century Renaissance* (London, 1969)

BROOKE, R. B. *Early Franciscan Government* (Cambridge, 1959)

CABROL, F. and LECLERQ, H. *Dictionnaire d'archéologie chrétienne et de liturgie* (Paris, 1907 sqq.)

CONANT, K. J. *Benedictine Contributions to Church Architecture* (Latrobe, Pa., 1949)

    Carolingian and Romanesque Architecture 800–1200, 2nd ed. (Harmondsworth, 1966)

CRANAGE, D. H. S. *The Home of the Monk* (Cambridge, 1926; 3rd ed. 1934)

CROSS, F. L. (ed.) *Oxford Dictionary of the Christian Church* (London, 1957)

DIMIER, A. *Les Moines bâtisseurs* (Paris, 1964)

DODWELL, C. R. (ed.) Theophilus, *De Diversibus Artibus* (London, 1961)

    Painting in Europe 800–1200 (Harmondsworth, 1971)

EGBERT, V. W. *The Mediaeval Artist at Work* (Princeton, 1967)

ESCHAPASSE, M. *L'Architecture bénédictine en Europe* (Paris, 1963)

EVANS, J. *Monastic Life at Cluny, 910–1157* (London, 1931)

    The Romanesque Architecture of the Order of Cluny (Cambridge, 1938)

    Cluniac Art of the Romanesque Period (Cambridge, 1950)

GODFREY, J. *The Church in Anglo-Saxon England* (Cambridge, 1962)

GOUGAUD, L. *Christianity in Celtic Lands* (London, 1932)

GRABAR, A. and NORDENFALK, C. *Early Medieval Painting* (Lausanne, 1957)

    Romanesque Painting (Lausanne, 1958)

HAHN, H. *Die frühe Kirchenbaukunst der Zisterzienser* (Berlin, 1957)

HARVEY, J. H. *The Gothic World, 1100–1600. A Survey of architecture and art* (London, 1950; paperback New York, 1969)

HENRY, F. *Irish Art in the Early Christian Period (to 800 A.D.)*, rev. ed. (London, 1965)

KNOWLES, D. *The Religious Orders in England*, 3 vols. (Cambridge, 1948–59)

    The Monastic Order in England, 2nd ed. (Cambridge, 1963)

    From Pachomius to Ignatius (Oxford, 1966)

    Christian Monasticism (London, 1969)

KRAUTHEIMER, R. *Die Kirchen der Bettelorden in Deutschland* (Cologne, 1925)

LAMBERT, E. *L'Architecture des Templiers* (Paris, 1955)

LEVISON, W. *England and the Continent in the Eighth Century* (Oxford, 1946)

LONGHI, L. F. DE *L'Architettura delle chiese cisterciensi italiane* (Milan, 1958)

MICHELI, G. L. *La Miniature du haut moyen-âge et les influences irlandaises* (Brussels, 1939)

MOORMAN, J. *A History of the Franciscan Order* (Oxford, 1968)

NASH-WILLIAMS, E. *Early Christian Monuments of Wales* (Cardiff, 1952)

NORMAN, E. R. and ST JOSEPH, J. K. S. *The Early Development of Irish Society* (Cambridge, 1969)

OURSEL, C. *La Miniature du XIIᵉ siècle à l'abbaye de Cîteaux* (Dijon, 1926) *Miniatures cisterciennes* (Dijon, 1960)

PANOFSKY, E. *Abbot Suger on the Abbey Church of St-Denis and its Art Treasures* (Princeton and London, 1946)

PENCO, G. *Storia del monachesimo in Italia dalle origini alla fine del Medio Evo* (Rome, 1961)

PORCHER, J. *French Miniatures from Illuminated Manuscripts* (London, 1959)

PORTER, A. K. *Romanesque Sculpture of the Pilgrimage Roads.* 10 vols. (Boston, 1923)

PUIG I CADAFALCH, J. *La Géographie et les origines du premier art roman* (Paris, 1935)

RICKERT, M. *Painting in Britain: the Middle Ages* (Harmondsworth, 1954)

RYAN, J. *Irish Monasticism, Origins and Early Development* (Dublin, 1931)

SABATIER, P. *Life of St Francis of Assisi*, trs. by L. S. Houghton (London, 1894)

SACKUR, E. *Die Cluniacenser*, 2 vols. (Halle, 1892–4)

SCHMIDT, PH. *Histoire de l'ordre de saint Benoît*, 7 vols. (Gembloux, 1942–56)

SHERLEY-PRICE, L. S. *Francis of Assisi. His life and writings as recorded by his Contemporaries* (London, 1959)

SWARTWOUT, R. E. *The Monastic Craftsman* (Cambridge, 1932)

TALBOT, C. H. *The Life of Christina of Markyate, a Twelfth Century Recluse* (Oxford, 1959)

VAUGHAM, R. *Matthew Paris* (Cambridge, 1958)

WORMALD, F. *The Monastic Library* (reprinted from *The English Library before 1700*, University of London, 1958, pp. 15 ff)

Sources of Illustrations

Where appropriate, manuscript references are given in brackets after the illustration number

Aachen, Suermondt-Museum **76**; Aerofilms **62**; Alinari **34, 35, 64, 100**; James Austin **27**; Azad **97**; Gerard Bakker **44**; Bamberg, Staatsbibliothek **8** (MS Patr. 61, f. 29v), **22** (MS Misc. Lit. 1, f. 126v); Berlin, Kupferstichkabinett **85**, Staatliche Bildstelle **98**; Brogi **104**; CAF **31**; Cambridge, Corpus Christi College, courtesy the Master and Fellows **114** (MS 4, f. 241v), Trinity College, courtesy the Master and Fellows **53** (bound in with MS R. 17. 1), **111** (MS R. 17. 1, f. 24), University Library **66** (MS Dd. 1. 4, f. 220); Cambridge, Mass., Fogg Art Museum, bequest of Hervey E. Wetzel 1911 **102**; G. Chiolini **91**; CIM **61**; Cluny, Musée Ochier **52**; Professor Kenneth J. Conant **6, 48, 50**; John Dayton **93**; Dijon, Bibliothèque Municipale **56** (MS 130, f. 104), **67** (MS 158, f. 1v), **68** (MS 168, f. 4v), **69** (MS 15, f. 56v), **70** (MS 170, f. 59), **71** (MS 170, f. 75v), **72** (MS 173, f. 41), **73** (MS 129, f. 4v), **74** (MS 641, f. 40v), Musée Archéologique **87**; Dublin, Trinity College **21** (f. 191v), **119** (MS E. 140, f. 61); Durham, Cathedral Library, courtesy the Dean and Chapter **115** (MS B. II. 13, f. 102), University, Department of Archaeology **16**; Florence, Biblioteca Medicea Laurenziana **3** (Plut. 12. 17, f. 3v), **20** (MS Amiat. 1, f. V), Soprintendenza alle Gallerie **103**; Hildesheim, St Godehard Library **86**, Magdalenkirche **123**; Hirmer Fotoarchiv München **33, 36, 43, 59**; Loïc-Jahan **4**; London, British Museum *frontispiece* (Harley Roll Y. 6), **2** (Arundel MS 155, f. 9v), **12** (Arundel MS 155, f. 133), **14** (Cotton MS Vesp. A. I, f. 30v), **19** (Cotton MS Nero D. IV, f. 25v), **28** (Add. MS 11662), **29** (Add. MS 49598, f. 102v), **83** (Cotton MS Dom. A. XVII, f. 73v), **84** (Add. MS 39843, f. 6v), **88, 120** (Roy. MS 2, B. VII, f. 177), **121** (Roy. MS 10. E. IV, f. 187), **126** (Cotton MS Nero D. I, f. 146v), Courtauld Institute of Art **13, 32, 38, 41, 51, 54, 60, 66, 94, 95, 106, 114, 115**, National Buildings Record **18**, Victoria and Albert Museum **108**, Warburg Institute **86**; Ian Mackenzie-Kerr **107**; Marburg **26, 40, 122**; Mas **37, 42, 46**; Naples, Biblioteca Nazionale **5** (Cod. VIII. C. 4); Werner Neumeister **39, 49**; New York, Pierpont Morgan Library **117** (MS M. 429, f. 183); Oxford, Bodleian Library **77, 78** (MS Douce 40, f. 36v), **79** (MS Laud. Misc. 409, f. 3v); Paris, Archives Photographiques **55, 75, 82**, Bibliothèque Nationale **47** (MS lat. 17716, f. 91), **101** (MS lat. 1176, f. 132), Musée des Monuments Français **92**; Prague, University Library **109** (MS XIV. A. 17, f. 16v); Rhodes, Istituto Storico Archeologico **91**; Jean Roubier **45, 65**; St Gallen, Stiftsbibliothek **11, 24** (redrawn); J. K. S. St Joseph **10, 80**; St Omer, Bibliothèque Municipale **29** (MS 56, f. 35); San Marino, Calif., Henry E. Huntington Library and Art Gallery **99**; Santiago de Compostela, Cathedral Library **42** (f. 162v); Edwin Smith **17, 81**; Sociedad Arqueológica Luliana **57**; Alan Sorrell **23**; Stockholm, Kungliga Biblioteket **15** (MS A. 135, f. 9v), **116** (MS A. 144, f. 34v); Utrecht, Rijksuniversiteit **110** (Script. eccl. 484, f. 8); Vatican Library **7** (MS Barb. lat. 592); Vienna, Kunsthistorisches Museum **9**; Washington, National Gallery of Art **126**; Winchester, Cathedral Library, courtesy the Dean and Chapter **112** (f. 131), **113** (f. 148); Yan **58, 96**; Professor George Zarnecki **38**. **25** is from Paul Petou, *De Nithardo Caroli Magni nepote . . .*, Paris 1613; **89** from G. S. Davies, *Charterhouse in London*, London (John Murray) 1921; **118** from E. and J.-G. Rott, *Hortus Deliciarum*, 1945; and **124** from M. A. Lenoir, *Architecture monastique*, Paris 1852–6.

Index